Praise for

Business Models for Financial Advisors

by Christine Timms

"The ideas and templates Chris developed in *Business Models for Financial Advisors* are useful and practical. Advisors like myself can benefit immensely by using these tools to help structure our practice and therefore provide a more consistent and positive client experience."

—Maili Wong, CFA, CFP®, FEA
Executive Vice-President, Senior Investment Advisor & Senior Portfolio Manager, Director, Wellington-Altus Holdings Inc.
Named one of Canada's Most Powerful Women: Top 100™ by WXN
Author of *Smart Risk: Invest Like The Wealthy To Achieve A Work-Optional Life*

"*Business Models for Financial Advisors* has been a valuable source of ideas and tools for my practice. The service model (communications, investing, tax, resource management, pricing/client cost) checklists provided us with documented questions on areas we may have thought of previously but have never written down as a defined process. It created awareness that we may not be going as deep into personalizing meetings for each client. My associate specifically found the financial planning service model helpful. Along with our current model, he appreciates the detail put into the checklists. I think they would be a major asset for advisors that lack process and a huge asset for advisors early in a career."

—Kevin Punshon
Financial Advisor for over 30 years
Chairman's Club member
Branch Manager
Big Five Canadian Bank owned brokerage firm

CT
Financial.

Handbooks for the
Professional Financial Advisor

Business Models
for
Financial Advisors

---

*Develop and Articulate Your
Unique Business Model*

Christine Timms

Paperback ISBN: 978-1-7773145-8-3
French Flap Paperback ISBN: 978-1-7773145-9-0
ePub ISBN: 978-1-7773453-0-3
MOBI ISBN: 978-1-7773453-1-0
PDF ISBN: 978-1-7773453-5-8

Published by CT Financial Press

Cover design by CT Financial Press & Melissa Levesque

Edited by Kristen Silva

Refer to www.ChristineTimms.com to buy handbooks and templates from the "Handbooks for the Professional Financial Advisor" series

I dedicate this book to my father, Reginald (Rex) Timms,
who inspired my attention to detail and encouraged my ambition.

Contents

Introduction to the Handbooks for the Professional Financial Advisor Series

I see myself as a client advocate who believes the best way to help financial services clients is to help the advisors who give independent financial advice. For the purposes of this series, I will define a financial advisor as an individual looking to provide services relating to investments, financial planning and/or insurance to individuals and small businesses. I believe that clients are best served by continuous long-term relationships with human advisors who seek to understand and work with the client to achieve the client's goals. The following quote from a note I received from a couple upon my retirement confirms that belief:

> *"In wishing you the best, we want to thank you and your team for looking after our investments so well over the last 20 years. With a high level of professionalism, you have guided us through good times and bad with the consistent proven good advice to 'stay the course'. Throughout, you have communicated openly, proactively and reviewed and reported on our circumstances consistently. Not only did you provide guidance with our investment portfolio but also took the time to advise us in the overlapping areas of tax issues, insurance benefits, estate planning and will preparation. Lastly our yearly reviews were not only extremely helpful but cemented the personal relationships. Thank you!"*
>
> —retired couple

I believe that by helping advisors succeed, I will help financial services clients succeed. I am also hoping that management of advisor firms, regulators and industry product/service suppliers will read these handbooks to gain a deeper awareness of the uniqueness and needs of both advisors and advisors' clients.

A financial advisor's job has always been stressful due to the unpredictability of financial markets and the people issues of any service industry. I believe the job is even more difficult today because of increased competition, the expansion of potential services (financial planning, etc.) and the growing number of investments available as well as increasing regulatory requirements. The good news is that advisors who use constantly evolving fintech and processes to improve their services and efficiency are able to increase the capacity and profitability of their practice while making advice available to more people.

I have written these handbooks to coach and assist advisors hoping to help reduce their stress and increase their productivity. I present ideas and processes relating to all aspects of a financial services practice with an emphasis on services, organization and preparedness. Preparedness reduces the stress of encounters with clients, prospects, markets, etc. Having a clearly articulated business plan, sharing the workload with a team and having a succession plan in place all work to reduce the stress of the business while making it easier to serve more clients effectively and profitably. The ideas are intended to help all advisors regardless of their unique approach to investing and client service, their unique clientele and their practice size. I hope to make it easier for advisors to serve their clients well, to the benefit of all stakeholders in a strong, sustainable financial advice industry (clients, advisors, advisors' firms, product providers).

As you might expect, this means sharing my experiences from my 33-year career as a financial advisor and showing what I learned from my mistakes. However, it also means sharing many templates and calculators (downloadable from my website) to help advisors easily implement the ideas that I share. During my career, I attended many practice management seminars agreeing with much of the advice given, but failing to implement the ideas because it would take too much time to do so. I am going to provide templates and calculators using my practice as an example, but I fully expect advisors to edit, modify and customize them to match their personal approach and the needs of their unique clientele. My customizable templates will help an advisor implement the ideas quickly as it is much easier to edit, modify and customize than it is to create from scratch.

> *"I really like your approach and, in particular, all the useful templates and checklists you provide. It is far more practical than many practice management books I have read over the 32 years I have been in the industry."*
>
> —Gary Mayzes
> Senior management of a Big Five Canadian Bank

I have been asked if these handbooks are intended to be "best practices for financial advisors." I hope they are "good practices for financial advisors" handbooks. I can't possibly claim "best" practices as I know there are many techniques and processes created by many advisors and/or firms that I am not even aware of.

I enjoyed helping many advisors over the years, sometimes formally under a firm inspired mentor program and sometimes through seminars sanctioned by management. However, most of my mentoring was "ad hoc" primarily for advisors within my own firm whom I met at conferences or within my own branch. These books are an opportunity to provide more complete and thorough mentoring for more financial advisors with practices in all financial services channels ranging from the large bank dealer to the financial planner operating as a sole practitioner.

> *"I have been in the business for 25+ years working in various management roles. I have worked with many investment advisors in my career and must tell you from a 'client first mindset', Chris is one of the best. ... We could all learn a thing or two from Chris."*
>
> —Wilma Ditchfield
> Senior management of a Big Five Canadian Bank

Handbooks in the Series

As I write this introduction to my series of handbooks for financial advisors, I have essentially completed handbooks regarding business models, team building, and transitioning clients and the retirement exit decision. I expect to complete another handbook about presentations and processes in the near future.

These books will reflect my strong belief that the "win-win" approach builds happier, sustainable relationships with all the stakeholders of your practice (clients, team members, branch management, service/product providers and senior firm management). The win-win concept does not mean that you compromise your own benefits but rather you grow the size of the pie to be shared so that all parties receive more—it is winning alongside each of the other stakeholders of your practice.

I recommend reading the entire series of handbooks once even though some areas may not seem immediately applicable to your practice. For example, you may think you are too young to consider the chapters relating to retirement or transitioning a clientele; however, you are likely not too young to think about pursuing a group referral of clients from another advisor. An advisor approaching retirement may initially see no need to read the business models handbook; however, upon reading it, they will see how they can easily articulate and compare their business model to that of the appropriate successor advisor. I have provided a detailed table of contents in each book to provide a quick overview and to help you easily refer to specific topics as the need arises over time.

Business Models for Financial Advisors

> *"You have set a great example for others running a very strong and successful practice.... I always knew your clients were very well taken care of."*
>
> —Steve Geist
> Former Group Head - Wealth Management
> Canadian Imperial Bank of Commerce

A well-articulated, written business model is a valuable tool for advisors at all stages of their career. An Advisor's deeper understanding of their own practice and who it serves best, will lead to sustainable relationships based on a win-win business model. I will define an advisor's business model as the articulation of who the advisor's most compatible clients are, the services and products that the advisor offers those clients, how those products/services are provided, how clients are charged and how the advisor is paid. I show how advisors in all stages of their careers can benefit from a well-defined business model, even those about to retire. The handbook provides a checklist process to quickly articulate, develop or analyze an existing or desired unique business model. I provide an example of the process by showing completed checklists based on the final years of my practice and the resulting printed business model. I include discussions regarding many of the required decisions as we progress through the checklists for the various business model components. I also discuss household capacity of practices and provide an analytical tool and checklists to facilitate the segmentation of clientele. This handbook includes appendices "Why Advisors are Not Interchangeable", "Why Many Full-Service Independent Revenue Sharing Advisors Have and Deserve Above Average Incomes" and "The Average Advisor of Various Financial Advice Channels."

Team Building for Financial Advisors

> *"Chris always seemed to gather people around that seemed to know what they were doing, they were young and learning the business, but they always struck me as being competent. But more than that, they seem to recognize the interests of the client, and they look after the client just as well as Chris does. In other words, they reflected her."*
>
> —Dennis Dack (client of 30 years)
> Retired Director of Strategic Policy
> Advisor to the Chairman of the Board
> Ontario Hydro

My team played a huge part in my overall success. I believe that my business would have plateaued at about 20% of my final practice (assets under management and revenue) if I had not built a team. This handbook focuses on the benefits of team building, delegating, supervising, outsourcing, hiring, training, team structure, compensation, motivation, turnover, etc. Team building is another classic example of a win-win approach to business. All of the stakeholders in an advisor's practice (clients, team members, advisor and firm) win from the advisor's ability to work with and delegate to team members. My willingness to build and nurture a team allowed me to expand my service to existing clients and pursue more clients resulting in a bigger and happier clientele, which naturally produced more revenue to be shared by myself, my team members and my firm.

Transitioning Clients and the Retirement Exit Decision

> *"Chris cared and continues to care about her clients - absolutely evident in her approach to her team and her solid plan for her retirement and the transition of her clients to the RIGHT advisors. The final proof is her two successors' very high client retention rate three years after her retirement."*
>
> —Wilma Ditchfield
> Senior management of a Big Five Canadian Bank

I retired with the largest assets under management and highest annual revenue of my career. I believe this was partially due to high client retention in my later years as clients were aware of my succession plans years before I actually announced my retirement. Three years after my retirement the assets and revenue generated from the clients transitioned to my successors were higher than when I left.

The handbook contains three interrelated topics:

1) Seeking Group Referrals from Another Advisor
2) Transitioning Your Clientele to Your Successor
3) The Retirement Exit Decision

The need to transition clients from one advisor to another advisor can be triggered by many different circumstances. An advisor will make group referrals to a successor advisor when they are retiring, reducing their clientele or changing their business model. The key to a successful transition of clients is compatibility between the successor, referring advisor and the clientele being referred. I believe this compatibility is more likely to be achieved when the successor and the referring advisor understand each other's positions and business models. Reading all three topics will provide the reader with needed insight and understanding in addition to providing step-by-step processes and tools to complete the transition.

Deciding when to retire is a very personal decision. I give my own reasons in "Why I Retired" as well as what I enjoy most about being retired. In "Hints That It May Be Time to Start Preparing for Retirement", I have provided a list of possible reasons for retiring that I have experienced or learned from others in the financial advice industry. I then point out many of the personal and business dangers of waiting too long to retire. Finally, I outline several steps that I recommend in preparation for an advisor's retirement.

Future Handbook on Processes and Presentations

I have gathered much of the content but have yet to complete the handbook relating to processes and presentations. This book will provide a lot of the "nuts and bolts" needed to implement an advisor's business model. Our presentations and interactions with clients showed them that we understood them and their needs making it easier for clients to trust us and understand our advice. The use of systematic processes and templates by yourself and your team will enable efficient delegation and supervision of the performance of many of the activities needed to find and service your sustainable client base and help you run your practice. During my career, my team and I developed many detailed presentations and processes including templates, calculators and macros for all six of the business model components with an emphasis on the major categories of the service model. These processes along with a good contact management system (client relationship management software or CRM) allowed me to grow my clientele and expand both my team and services. This handbook will discuss processes and presentations in great detail for each business model component and provide tools and templates to help advisors easily implement and customize the ideas that appeal to them.

I hope these handbooks leave advisors with a lot to think about, some ideas relevant to their practice and the means to implement those ideas.

> *"I have found all three of these books to be very thought provoking, not only as it relates to the information provided, but also from looking forward within the context of my own practice and my own personal plan for the next stage of my life."*
> —Rollie Guenette
> Financial Advisor for over 25 years
> Chairman's Club member
> Big Five Canadian bank owned brokerage firm

Business Models

for

Financial Advisors

Introduction

A well-thought-out and articulated business model will give a financial advisor the focus needed to efficiently and effectively provide the services they deem appropriate for their chosen client base.

For the purposes of this book, I will define an advisor's business model as the articulation of who the advisor's most compatible clients are, the services and products that the advisor offers/provides to those clients, how those products/services will be provided, how clients are charged and how the advisor is paid. Advisors in all stages of their careers can benefit from a well-defined business model ... even those about to retire.

During my 33 years as an advisor, I met many advisors with long successful careers. I learned that no two advisors are exactly alike. They all have distinguishing characteristics, different skill sets and different clienteles. Each advisor employs different combinations of successful and valid approaches to client contact, investing, financial planning, charging clients, etc. The successful advisor's approach to the services offered generally matches the needs of the advisor's unique clientele. There may be almost as many unique business models as there are advisors. From a client's point of view, finding a truly compatible advisor is a challenge. A good relationship is to be cherished and protected. Clients should have the right and opportunity to develop a long-term relationship with such an advisor. Trusting relationships take time to develop and are not readily interchangeable. "Appendix A: Why Advisors are Not Interchangeable" explains this in detail.

The Evolution of my Unique Business Model

When I began as an advisor, I was 26 years old. I was well educated with a Math degree, an accounting designation, industry courses and a well respected four-month training program provided by Merrill Lynch. I had no ready-made clients from my previous profession or personal life and had not yet fully developed my views toward how to invest or how to serve clients. In the beginning I had no business model. I was trying to be all things to all people. In my first two years in the business, I was willing to experiment with whatever my clients suggested even if it involved speculative investments. I remember feeling that I was more conservative than most advisors, and I wanted to invest clients' serious money, not speculate with their play money. If I had continued to let a few speculator clients distract me and dominate my time, my practice would have stagnated as other clients and prospects received less attention.

Gradually, my "business model" became an ad hoc collection of ideas based on what I knew about myself and what I was comfortable recommending to clients. These ideas accumulated and evolved as my knowledge and experiences grew. I had not fully formulated my approach to investing, but I knew that I wanted to minimize volatility and give my clients peace of mind. I also knew that I wanted my client's portfolios to be well diversified and include investments from outside Canada. As the years passed, I discovered services and products to add by exploring new developments in the industry and by listening to individual client's needs and realizing that many of my other clients shared the same needs. As I look back on my career, I realize that I gradually made groups of interrelated decisions that formed an unarticulated, unwritten business model that was best for myself and the clients I wished to serve. I can see now that the more business model decisions I made, the more focused and efficient my practice became. I had removed the stress of trying to be all things to all people, giving me greater peace of mind. I am confident that I would have arrived at my final business model and all of its benefits sooner if I had used a written business model development process similar to the checklist process I have designed and described for advisors in this handbook.

The purpose of this handbook is to encourage and help advisors articulate, develop or refine their unique business model with an easily produced written version that they will be comfortable showing to others. The process of creating the business model will also serve as a tool to assist in marketing and practice management. I will:

1) Describe the benefits of developing and having a written business model for advisors at all stages of their career.

2) Show how non-advisory industry participants can benefit by understanding the components of financial advisors' business models.

3) Discuss the components of an advisor's business model (compatible clientele, communication methods, investing, financial planning, tax, resources, pricing, compensation, etc.) and the many alternatives that must be considered as an advisor develops their own unique model.

4) Provide a listing of many potential actions or items in each of those business model components in checklist format.

5) Provide a thought process for developing each component of a unique business model using the personal experiences of myself and others to assist advisors in the creation of their own business model. I offer my final practice as an example of a completed checklist.

6) Provide advisors with a quick and easy template of checklists and macros downloadable through my website to create, modify and/or articulate their own unique written business model.

Advisors in All Stages of Their Careers Benefit from a Well-Defined Business Model

A well-articulated, written business model is a valuable tool for advisors at all stages of their career. Advisors having a deeper understanding of their own practice and who it serves best, will lead to sustainable relationships based on a win-win business model.

Future Advice Industry Participants

Individuals considering a career in financial advice who read this book will gain an understanding of an advisor's many possible approaches to providing services through the business model checklists and discussions. This will enable them to make better informed career path decisions regarding their initial position (advisor, team member, or non-advisor industry participant), their choice of financial advice channel, their preferred method of compensation (salary vs revenue sharing), the firm and/or the particular advisor's practice they choose to join. An aspiring advisor will likely find "Appendix C: The Average Advisor of Various Financial Advice Channels" helpful, as well as the checklist for the advisor compensation component as it includes advisor career goals, desired responsibilities, sources of advisor enjoyment and satisfaction, personal qualities and skill sets. Individuals considering joining an advisor's team will likely also benefit from my *Team Building for Financial Advisors* handbook.

Team Members (Assistants and Associates)

The assistants and associates of an advisor who read their advisor's unique business model will gain an understanding of who the advisor's most compatible clients are, the services and products that the advisor offers/provides those clients, how those products/services are provided, how clients are charged and how the advisor is paid. The team members' individual tasks will have more meaning when they understand the purpose of their activity in the context of the overall business model.

New Advisors

This book will lead new advisors through the process of developing their initial business model. It will help them identify suitable and compatible prospective clients and lead them through a decision process to choose which services they wish to offer. It will also help them decide how to charge clients and how they wish to be paid (salary vs revenue sharing). The discussions regarding the processes to deliver these services will be found in my future handbook about processes and presentations for clients and prospects.

Established Advisors

> *"The ideas and checklists presented in this book are very timely and helpful for us to use as a business planning tool as we develop and settle our business plan forward and develop the appropriate business model(s) to help us accomplish our objective.... It is, in aggregate, a superb tool for us to use to help all of the people in my practice determine, define and settle the forward direction we need to take our business to the next higher level."*
>
> —Rollie Guenette
> Financial Advisor for over 25 years
> Chairman's Club member
> Big Five Canadian Bank owned brokerage firm

Most established advisors will have a basic business model in their head (it may involve being all things to all people) but won't have written it down. Even when their business model is very clear and focused in the advisor's mind, there are definite advantages to having it written down and easily conveyed to others. A well-articulated, written business model is a valuable tool that can assist in many aspects of a financial advice practice including marketing, prospecting for clients, pursuing referrals from clients and centres of influence, team building and training, choosing contact management and financial planning software, choosing a firm, determining household capacity, etc. It will also help an advisor identify the criteria for their most sustainable relationships and help them search for a successor for some or all of their clientele. The advisor who is struggling, or who is looking to take their practice to a higher level, will also benefit from this book's discussions around the many decisions/choices involved in developing a unique business model. It can help them refine the focus of their practice for efficiency and stimulate ideas to improve service to their most compatible clients who appreciate and are willing to pay for the services the advisor is happy to offer. A well-thought-out business model will help advisors with the challenge of providing the appropriate level of service for each client while minimizing the use of the advisor's resources.

Upon implementing a written business model, it will be easier for an advisor to stop trying to be "all things to all people". An advisor will be able to focus their ongoing learning on topics relevant to a significant number of their clients. It will be easier to choose the most relevant industry courses. It will also be easier to apply what is learned from finding a solution for one client to other clients facing similar situations. As a result, the advisor will become more proficient in the services offered and in promoting their services to prospects. All the advisor's clients will benefit, and the advisor will maximize the effectiveness of their time and money invested in their career/practice. A well-articulated business model will give added confidence to an advisor helping them project confidence to existing and prospective clients. It will also provide structure and facilitate the delegation of duties to team members as the advisor's practice grows. A well-thought-out written business model should lead to happier clients as well as more enjoyable and productive workdays for the advisor and their team. A win-win!

Advisors Pursuing Referrals from Retiring/Downsizing Advisors
Many advisors today aspire to take over the clienteles of retiring advisors or partial clienteles of advisors wishing to refer a group of their clients. A retiring/referring advisor and the advisor's firm will want to maximize client retention by finding a successor advisor who is compatible with the clients being referred. A potential successor's written business model describing the successor advisor's existing clientele and the services provided to those clients—including the methods of client contact, the approach to investing and financial planning as well as how clients are charged—will go a long way to determining the successor advisor's compatibility with the retiring advisor's clients. The business model will also help the potential successor prepare a service plan for integrating new clients into their practice. The level of professionalism indicated by a written business model and integration plan should build the referring advisor and management's confidence in the potential successor's ability to successfully transition the referred clients. This confidence will increase the chances of being chosen as a successor. The *Transitioning Clients and the Retirement Exit Decision* handbook in this series is dedicated to assisting both the retiring/downsizing advisor and successor advisor work through the successful transition of clients between advisors.

Advisors Approaching Retirement
An advisor approaching retirement will need to search for an appropriate successor to take over serving their clients unless they have at least one team member who is willing and capable of assuming their role. While writing the *Transitioning Clients and the Retirement Exit Decision* handbook of this series, I realized how valuable a detailed written business model would

be to both the retiring/downsizing advisor and the successor advisor in the process of a successful transition of clients between advisors. A written business model will describe a practice's clientele and include the methods of client contact, the approach to investing and financial planning and how clients are charged. A comparison of the retiring and potential successor advisor practices' written business models should help the retiring advisor choose the right successor. The right successor will not necessarily have the same business model as the retiring advisor but will have the business model that the retiring advisor believes will be best for the future. For example, a retiring advisor may believe that a fee-based and/or managed money practice is best for the future even if their practice is currently based on commissions and/or stock picking. The retiring advisor's written business model will also help the successor understand the referred client's experiences and expectations of their new advisor. Many older advisors will have modified their business model in their head over the years, but most have not written it down.

———

Most advisors are unlikely to create a written business model because of the time it would take to do so from scratch. This book provides a quick and organized process for creating a written business model through the use of customizable checklists and macros. (The checklists can be found on my website.) Using these checklists to simply record the business model of an existing practice will be fairly quick, while using the checklists to stimulate thoughts of developing or modifying a plan will take as long as the advisor's thought process needs.

Non-Advisor Industry Participants Benefit from Understanding Advisor's Business Models

Advisor firm management, regulators and industry product/service suppliers will gain a deeper awareness of the uniqueness and needs of both advisors and advisors' clients from a thorough understanding of the components of advisors' unique business models.

The financial advice industry is very unique, in that a successful advisor's most rewarding career path is usually to remain an advisor who grows and maintains their practice until retirement. The long careers of financial advisors are very beneficial to clients seeking long-term relationships with their advisors; however, it has resulted in a lack of experienced financial advisors in the non-advisor roles, such as firm management, regulators and industry product suppliers. This book is written for and from the perspective of the practicing financial advisor. However, I believe that advisor firm management, regulators and industry product/service suppliers will gain a deeper awareness of the uniqueness and needs of both advisors and advisors' clients from a thorough understanding of the components of advisors' unique business models as explained in this book and appendices.

Advisor Firm Management
Over the last few decades, much of the financial advice industry has gradually been absorbed into larger financial institutions. As a result, the senior management and managers of advisors are less likely to have the hands-on experience of a practicing financial advisor. A thorough understanding of the components

of advisors' unique business models will help management maintain and develop win-win policies that promote sustainable long-term relationships between firms, advisors and clients. Appendix A and Appendix B will add additional insight into what clients look for and appreciate in their financial advisor.

Advisor Firm Support for Advisors and Their Teams
There are many people within a full-service firm who are expected to support advisors and their teams. Many advisors are frustrated with their firm's support staff's lack of understanding of both advisor and client needs. A more thorough understanding of advisor business model components will help support staff relate to advisor and client needs resulting in better service to the advisors and their clients. I have listed below some examples of such firm support roles:

– Branch Administrators
– Back Office
– Compliance Officers
– Marketing
– Advisor Training and Education
– Technology
– Human Resources
– Research

Advisor Regulators
Regulators are populated primarily by lawyers and very few individuals with the hands-on experience of a practicing financial advisor. This is not surprising because of the legal component of creating and enforcing regulations. Unfortunately, most advisors are reluctant to volunteer candid opinions to regulators, likely due to advisors' natural skepticism, fear of reprisal and focus on serving their clients' everyday needs. I believe this book should help the regulators put themselves in the shoes of an advisor and therefore be better equipped to ensure that the long-term

interests of the client and the advisor are naturally aligned, a win-win for everyone.

Advisors' Suppliers/Partners

If you are looking to sell products to or receive referrals from financial advisors, reading this book will help you understand some of an advisor's decision-making processes and enable you to determine how your product/service can fit into an advisor's unique business model. I have listed below some examples of such suppliers and partners:

- Money management firms of mutual funds, separately managed accounts (SMAs), ETFs, etc.
- Life insurance companies
- Contact management system providers
- Financial planning software providers
- Investment portfolio software providers
- Referral partners (bankers, trust officers, lawyers, accountants)
- Lead generators

— — —

Essentially, I think this book should be helpful to anyone working or aspiring to work in or with the financial advice industry.

Components of a Financial Advisor's Unique Business Model

There are many potential financial advisor business models in the financial advice industry. Advisors of today have a lot more to choose from and many more decisions to make than I did when I was starting out. Frankly, the number of alternatives can be overwhelming and distracting. As is usually the case, when faced with a significant challenge, it is best to break it down into a series of smaller, more manageable steps.

Determine Your Overall Mission and Commitment to Clients

The first step in creating your unique business model is determining your overall mission and commitment to your clients. This mission should resonate and appeal to potential individuals or companies who you want to maintain and/or pursue as compatible and sustainable long-term clients. Your commitment to clients should reflect how the services provided and your processes accomplish your mission. Your business model is all about organizing your practice's services, processes, etc. to effectively and efficiently achieve your overall mission and fulfill your commitment to your clients. Every component and detail of your business model should be evaluated by you in relation to your overall mission and your commitment to your clients right down to the selection of each potential service, investment, etc. You may find yourself modifying your mission and/or your commitment when faced with the practicality of implementing your proposed business model. Your mission and commitment need to appeal to your compatible and sustainable clients as well as create an enjoyable, profitable practice for yourself, your team and your firm.

An Example: My Mission and Commitment to Clients

Our team's mission:
Very early in my career, I determined that my mission was to help clients achieve financial peace of mind.

Our team's commitment to our clients:
After reading the 100+ comments I received from my clients when I retired, I could see that my clients clearly appreciated the financial peace of mind that my team and I brought to them through our services and commitment to communication. The client comments ultimately reflected our unwritten commitment to our clients. I decided it was time (after 33 years in the business) to write down "Our commitment to our clients".

- We are committed to helping each of our clients achieve Financial Peace of Mind.

- We learn what Financial Peace of Mind means to each individual client.

- We employ a straightforward, easy to understand, disciplined approach to investing, designed to make it easier for clients to be patient in good times and bad.

- We work hard to present financial information and plans in easy to understand formats.

- We are very accessible to our clients. No question is a silly question.

- We don't want blind faith; we want our clients to understand the logic behind our advice and easily see for themselves that we are following through on our commitment to them.

I believe my prospecting and marketing efforts would have benefited by the above written articulation of this commitment. Eventually, my entire business model flowed from and contributed to our ultimate mission of each client's financial peace of mind. I have identified six major components of the financial advisor's business model.

Six Major Components of the Financial Advisor's Business Model

1. Identify the most compatible clients for your practice
Who do you, the advisor, wish to serve and what is the criteria that will most likely lead to a long-term sustainable relationship between you and the client?

2. Establish your unique client service model
What services/products do you wish to offer clients?

a. client communication

b. investing

c. financial planning

d. tax returns and tax strategies

3. Determine your processes for delivery of services/products and practice management
How will you implement your service model?

4. Determine needed resources and suppliers/sources
What resources are needed for the processes you use to deliver the services? What resources are readily available through your firm and external sources? How much of your own time and money is needed?

5. Determine pricing and client costs
How and how much should your clients pay for the services/products they receive (including direct and indirect costs)?

6. Evaluate advisor compensation and career paths
How do you wish to be paid: consistent earnings (salary) versus potential earnings (revenue sharing)?

The next portion of this handbook provides a process that lists and discusses many of the choices and decisions to be made within each of those components. My website provides downloadable customizable checklists for an advisor to create and/or articulate their unique business model.

A Checklist Process to Develop and/or Articulate an Advisor's Unique Business Model

I have created a process to provide an orderly progression through the various business model items available to financial advisors by expanding each of the six business model components into detailed checklists. The checklists can be used to quickly document, develop or analyze an existing or desired unique business model. This book provides an example of the process by showing completed checklists based on the final years of my practice and the resulting printed business model. This example has been modified and condensed from the templates provided on my website to fit formatting requirements of this book. I include discussions regarding many of the required decisions as we progress through the checklists for the various business model components.

To enable advisors to implement this process with minimal cost and effort, my website offers downloadable, customizable Excel spreadsheet templates of all the checklists discussed. They allow an advisor to add their own items and details to my ready-made lists. The process should be fairly quick to identify an established, existing business model while other purposes will take as long as the advisor's thought process requires.

> *"I really like your approach and, in particular, all the useful templates and checklists you provide. It is far more practical than many practice management books I have read over the 32 years I have been in the industry."*
>
> —Gary Mayzes
> Senior management of a Big Five Canadian Bank

Clarify Your Purpose Before You Start Completing Checklists

Before you start completing the checklists, you should clarify your purpose. I have listed some possible purposes below:

- Describe your existing business model (for use by advisor, team, management, potential successor, outsource partner, etc.).

- Describe the business model you aspire to in the near and/or distant future.

- Look to expand clientele or services. (Stimulate ideas you haven't considered before.)

- Look to reduce services. (Streamline your business by identifying and eliminating services that are used by very few clients.)

- Look to reduce the number of clients you serve. (Identify clients who don't fit your business model for a potential group referral to another advisor.)

- Evaluate potential software programs (contact management systems, financial planning programs, etc.).

- Identify services and resources needed from your firm.

Depending on your purpose, you may wish to fill some of the boxes in the checklists with further clarification instead of just an "X". For example, you may want to indicate what portion of your clientele the item applies to by inserting a percent value or "few" or "all". You should give your checklist a title reflecting the purpose and remember to keep the purpose in mind as you progress through the multiple checklists. An advisor might wish to create separate versions of the same checklist to satisfy different purposes.

Order of Completion of Checklists

The best order of completing these checklists may vary from the order I present, and depends on the individual advisor's current knowledge and convictions as well as the circumstances of their life and career. Many of the answers to the questions raised are affected by answers in the other checklists. If you are using the checklists to develop or modify a business model, I suggest reviewing all of the checklists relating to each of the business model components and checking the boxes you are most certain of first. For example, an experienced advisor may think they know their target market; but after honestly answering the questions relating to their service model, the advisor may realize that the services they intend to provide and enjoy providing don't match the preconceived target clientele needs.

Considerations During Completion of Checklists

As you complete the checklists, keep the following overall considerations in mind:

- Be very honest with yourself.
- You can't be everything to all people.
- You need to believe in the value of the services you offer.
- Don't offer a service that you don't enjoy providing unless you can outsource or delegate within your team with confidence.
- Don't assume that an entire checklist does not apply to you. For example, even if you do not produce financial plans, you may be providing some financial planning services.
- Although there is a special checklist for tax returns and tax strategies in the service component, tax considerations are sprinkled throughout all of the service model checklists.

Component 1: Identify the Most Compatible Clients for Your Practice

Identifying a suitable potential clientele is all about increasing the likelihood of compatibility between you and the prospective clients you pursue.

The purpose of the compatible client checklists is to help advisors avoid the mistakes I made when I pursued and accepted clients where a sustainable relationship was highly unlikely.

When I started in the business, I was eager to pursue and accept anyone who would agree to be my client. I found my clients one at a time, through cold-calling, walk-ins, call-ins, seminars and the occasional newspaper advertisement. Any list of names of people with phone numbers in my local area became my prospect list. Occasionally, I would also "inherit" an account from an advisor who left the firm. This lack of clarity regarding who my clients should be, was inefficient and led to my trying to be everything to everyone. I am sure it resulted in unnecessary client turnover. Eventually, I began to focus on investors who were saving for retirement with RRSPs, but this was still a very broad group of potential clients and resulted in a widely diversified clientele.

As I gained experience, I learned that my best, most appreciative clients and I were of "like mind". I found their life issues, priorities and goals easy to relate to and understand. They found me easy to trust and understand. In short … we were very compatible and liked each other. I became more comfortable cutting ties with clients who I found difficult to work with. As I gained confidence, I became better at identifying incompatible prospects early in the relationship and could stop myself from pursuing those prospects who would be difficult to work with. By the time I retired, I had reduced my clientele to highly compatible relationships and was losing only about 1% of my households per year.

An advisor is most likely to achieve long-lasting relationships with clients if they actively pursue clients who are compatible with them as a person and who can understand and appreciate the benefits of the services the advisor wishes to offer. Clearly, there is an infinite number of permutations and combinations of client circumstances, personalities and needs. No advisor can be compatible with all client personalities. Advisors need to find the clients who match up well with their personality, investment philosophy and service model to achieve long-term sustainable relationships.

I have developed a two-step checklist process to help an advisor identify the characteristics of potential and/or existing compatible clients where the relationships are most likely to be comfortable and mutually beneficial for a long time. The checklists will help newer advisors decide who to pursue as clients. They will help established advisors stand back and think about their existing client relationships and who they are most successful and happiest serving.

Step 1: Identify Compatible Groups of Clients and Potential Clients

Step 2: Identify Criteria for Sustainable Individual Relationships

The following sections provide the checklists for the two steps. As an example, I identify the most compatible and sustainable clients of the last several years of my practice with an "x". Some sections also include considerations for completing that section of the checklist and my personal insight into why I was successful with my identified compatible group or criteria.

An established advisor who wishes only to identify groups within their existing clientele will probably be able to complete the checklist quickly and then instantly produce their personal summary using the template downloadable from my website. An advisor whose purpose is more than identifying their existing clientele will likely take longer.

Step 1: Identify Compatible Groups of Clients and Potential Clients

The purpose of this checklist is to identify the commonalities of your best clients so you can serve them better and find more clients similar to them. When you have identified groups of people you appear most compatible with, you have also identified groups of prospects/leads that you are most likely to turn into long-term, mutually beneficial clients. Knowing these groups should help you narrow the focus of your marketing and/or cold-calling by helping you generate lists, etc. for more targeted prospecting campaigns. You will also have identified your most compatible clients who will likely send you the most compatible referrals, especially when you tell them you are looking for clients just like them. You should focus referral campaigns on your most compatible clients.

As you proceed through the checklist, keep in mind that you don't need to be part of a group to be compatible with the group. You do need to be able to relate to them and sincerely empathize with their situation and needs. Perhaps your family relationships and friendships have provided you with experiences leading to a good understanding and ability to empathize with the issues many of the group face. Also, if you are interested in focusing on a particular group, you may be able to find books or magazines that will aid in your understanding. For example, you don't have to be elderly to understand the elderly. You may have plenty of experience interacting with and helping elderly family members or friends and have discovered that you relate well to them and really enjoy the relationships. You can also choose to educate yourself regarding the concerns and needs of the elderly. For all the same reasons, you don't need be in a particular profession or business to understand and empathize with their concerns and needs. In any case, it is important that you recognize a compatibility with a group even if you don't know why the compatibility exists.

As promised, I will share completed sample checklists to identify potentially compatible groups based on the final years of my practice including my thoughts relating to each of the following categories:

- Professions/Occupations
- Business Owners and Organizations
- Background/Social Groups
- Common Beliefs
- Common Interests
- Age Groups
- Family Experiences
- Gender

Professions/Occupations

An advisor's prior work experience will often result in compatibility with those of the same profession/occupation. You might belong to the profession or, through personal experience, know that you are very comfortable with those that do. A good relationship with family members of particular professions may be an indication that you are very capable of empathizing with and understanding the needs of that group and therefore potentially compatible with that profession. Perhaps your existing relationships could give you insight into the group's wants and needs and why you may or may not be compatible with them. These relationships might also provide ideas regarding how to obtain contact information for individuals in those professions and occupations.

Professions/Occupations

x	business executives
x	lawyers
x	accountants
	doctors
	dentists
	pilots
	teachers/professors
	real estate agents
2 or 3	architects
< 10	engineers
	sports professionals
	trade: _____

Most of my earliest clientele consisted of business professionals because my initial prospect calling lists were professional directories and notices of promotions found in newspapers. The education and ambition of my younger self likely increased my compatibility with those groups, compensating for my lack of life experience. My compatibility with engineers probably came from living with my father, a civil engineer, and two brothers who became civil engineers. In hindsight, I should have searched for a directory of engineers for prospecting purposes, but I never thought of it. A checklist like this might have inspired me to do so.

Business Owners and Organizations

Many advisors who run their practice like a small business will naturally have a lot in common with small business owners and entrepreneurs. You may also be compatible with owners of businesses that serve your personal hobbies or where you have a sincere personal interest in the services they provide or the products they produce. If you have an interest in touring a client or prospect's plant or in viewing their product line, you may have compatibility if you can turn that interest into an understanding of their needs.

Business Owners and Organizations

x	any type of small business
	businesses supplying/making products you like: _____
	businesses providing services that interest you: _____
	businesses relating to your hobbies: _____
	businesses in your neighborhood: _____
	entrepreneurs
x	charitable foundations
x	proprietorships
x	medical professional corporations
x	trusts
x	holding companies

Although I had some success with charitable foundations, I found it difficult in some cases to sustain the relationships because of board member turnover. The same would be true of any organization where decision makers change regularly.

Background/Social Groups

Most individual advisors will relate well to groups who have a similar cultural background and/or share similar life experiences. A relatively unique ethnic or cultural background or knowledge of a particular language will give an advisor a significant advantage with that group of people. Your target/preferred clientele may be obvious to you based on your professional or personal background or pre-established relationships. For example, an advisor may have clients from a prior career in accounting who also need investment and financial planning advice.

Background/Social Groups

	advisor's ethnic background: _____
	familiar ethnic backgrounds: _____
	minority language: _____
	shared life experience (immigrant, war veteran, etc.)
x	small town
x	big city
	previous career peers
	clients from previous career

My experience of growing up in a small town in the Niagara region of Ontario and then moving to Toronto after university helped me relate well to both small town and big city residents.

Common Beliefs

People with common beliefs are likely to be compatible in a lot of ways; however, you must be very careful of how you approach this when pursuing potential clients. There is a danger of alienating a prospect and their circle of contacts if they think you are less interested in their cause than finding new clients. Any hint of insincerity will affect their ability to trust you. You definitely don't want to be seen as pretending empathy, as the apparent lack of sincerity will destroy trust.

Common Beliefs

	specific religious groups: _____
	political outlook: _____
	charitable causes: _____
	activist causes: _____

Common Interests

Common Interests

x	sports: __tennis__
x	vacation property: __cottage__
	fashion: _____
	art: _____
	theatre: _____
	music: _____
	use of social media: _____

Although I never prospected fellow tennis club members, I did gain a small number of clients when they learned more about me through our interactions at the club.

Age Group

Age Group

	teenager
	young adults
x	middle age
x	approaching retirement
>30%	early retirement
>20%	RRIF age 72+

I found that I was always comfortable working with clients who were middle-aged or older. They seemed to value my advice, and I found it easy relate to their needs. I would often delegate the relationships of younger generations to a younger team member who would likely be more compatible. Identifying your clients age groups might also help you focus your learning on subjects that will help them. For example, middle-aged professionals would have a greater need for disability insurance than the elderly.

Family Experiences

Your observations of family member experiences can open your eyes to potential services your family could have benefited from and inspire you to provide those services to your clients, thereby increasing your compatibility with a group even though you have not personally encountered the same situation.

Family Experiences

x	single
x	married
	divorced
x	widowed
x	big family
x	small family (only child)
x	caring for children
x	caring for the elderly
	caring for a disabled person

I found that the experience of caring and acting as power of attorney for my elderly mother helped me understand and empathize with elderly clients' day-to-day frustrations and personal issues as well as those issues affecting their finances. I was better able to identify with clients who were taking care of their elderly family members. I also found that having strong relationships with my siblings and their young children when I was single gave me more understanding of the issues of clients with growing families; although, I expect my siblings will tell you that my understanding grew more after I had a child of my own.

I was very successful with widows/widowers; although, I was not a widow and never pursued them as a group. Perhaps my compatibility grew as I gained experience through the existing clients who became widows/widowers and through referrals from existing clients.

Gender

	Gender
x	women
	men
	gay women
	gay men
	transgender

Individuals sharing your gender are likely more compatible; however, this is not always true and will depend on the individual. I remember an elderly woman who demanded that she be given a male advisor and was insulted that my manager had originally referred her to me, a female advisor, when her male advisor left.

Different Advisors Have Different Compatibility Prerequisites

An advisor will require different levels of compatibility for prospects at different stages of their career. An established advisor in a later stage of their career may require a short list of prospects where specific boxes have been checked. An advisor in a high growth stage of their career will need long lists of qualified prospects so they can call many people, one after another, to take the sting out of the many rejections they will inevitably face when they call a prospect without a previous introduction.

To be clear, I do not advocate turning away existing clients or referrals who are not in the identified compatible groups. The target groups are merely groups in which you are more likely to find compatible potential clients. Individual prospects and clients should be evaluated on an individual basis based on the criteria for sustainable relationships (step 2).

Step 2: Identify Criteria for Sustainable Individual Relationships

Once you have found individual prospects, either through lead generation or referral, each potential client-advisor relationship should be evaluated on an individual basis using the criteria for sustainable relationships. This should be accomplished initially through phone conversations or e-mails and then through meetings (usually face-to-face). This checklist will help you identify the criteria that will contribute to a sustainable relationship beneficial to both you and the client and therefore justify further pursuit of the prospect or keeping the client. I will show completed checklists based on the final years of my practice including my thoughts relating to each of the following categories to identify sustainable relationships:

- Personality Traits
- Client Goals
- Client Service Requirements
- Client's Comfort and Preferences Regarding Payment for Advice and Service
- Profitability: Immediate and Potential

Many prospective clients will be unsure of what they want and need, and will be open to the advisor's suggestions. Some of the personality traits, goals and service requirements of my long-time clients were nurtured by patient interactions and transparency with myself and my team. Sometimes you need time to find out if a client is compatible. Using the checklists should help an advisor evaluate whether expending the time and resources required to further pursue the relationship is worthwhile.

Personality Traits
People who genuinely like each other are generally more compatible, will enjoy working together, and are more likely to

maintain long relationships. Compatible personalities are not easy to define; and although most people seem to work best with people similar to themselves, sometimes the opposite is true. This checklist will help you identify the most common personality traits of clients you enjoy working with.

My longest and most successful relationships were with collaborative clients who were willing to share their thoughts and all of their information with me. They desired a long-term relationship with me and believed we should both benefit from the relationship. By the end of my career, most (maybe all) of my clients shared similar risk tolerances with me and were patient with volatile stock markets. Clients who wanted to take more risk than I was comfortable with were frustrated when I constantly cautioned against it, and they would usually move on to another advisor. We both would have been happier if we had realized our lack of compatibility earlier on.

Personality Traits

x	introvert
	extrovert
x	optimist
	cynical
x	humble/modest
x	confident
x	collaborative
x	appreciates long-term relationships
x	delegator
x	thankful
x	patient
	sense of humour
	ambitious
	high risk taker
x	moderate risk taker
x	conservative
x	ultra-conservative
	short-term focus
x	long-term focus

Client Goals

An advisor should be able to identify the client goals they are able to assist with. Clear identification of these goals will help the advisor explain their value added to existing and potential clients verbally and through marketing materials, websites, etc. You will need to know if your service models for investing and financial planning are likely to achieve the returns, etc. needed to satisfy the individual client's goals. Relationships will be most sustainable when the advisor can relate to the client's priorities in life. This checklist will help an advisor identify the goals that the advisor's service model can help clients achieve.

	Client Goals
x	protect family from loss of life/income
x	financial independence
x	retire comfortably
x	liquidity/access to capital
x	leave a legacy (heirs or charity)
	quick gains expected range of returns: _____
x	long-term gains expected range of returns: _6% - 10%_
x	fixed inc. expected return: _current 5yr GIC/gov't bond rates_
x	save for personal use real estate properties
x	maintain personal use real estate properties
	build rental real estate portfolio
x	plan for event (wedding or religious event)
x	spending/distributing wealth during lifetime
x	charitable giving during lifetime
x	train/teach their children
x	minimize tax
x	protect small business (personnel loss, marriage breakdown)
	small business succession planning

I found that many potential clients had not yet determined their long-term goals or stated their goals in terms of financial requirements. They needed me to help them set achievable short- and long-term goals.

Client Service Requirements

The definition of "reasonable" service expectations varies from client to client and advisor to advisor. The client's expectations should fall within your service model. You may have individual clients who are located outside your immediate area. Their need to be physically visited should be identified on the checklist below. Very few clients are worth going beyond the norm of your practice's service model and should meet many of your other criteria or be very important to justify it. Many potential clients do not know their service requirements because they are unfamiliar with what an advisor can offer and how they would benefit, so you and the clients will need to determine their needs together.

Client Service Requirements: Communication

x	accessible by phone
x	voicemail: _live person answers during office hours_
x	accessible by e-mail
	after business hours access to advisor
x	review meeting, advisor's office frequency: _annual_
x	review meeting, client's home/office frequency: _occasional_
x	out-of-town review meetings: _North Ontario town_
	virtual (screensharing) review frequency: _____
	virtual (camera) review meeting frequency: _____
x	minimum contact frequency: _annually_
x	maximum contact frequency: _weekly_
x	save/minimize client time requirements
	seminars and educational events
	invitations to entertainment events
x	written registered plan contribution reminders: _mail/e-mail_
x	call for registered plan contribution reminders

Service requirements of many clients will reduce over time as they gain understanding and confidence in the advisor and the advisor's approach to investing and service. I remember one client who started with me twenty years before I retired. For the first four years of our relationship, the client needed quarterly face-to-face meetings as well as regular phone calls. Within five to six years, she was only interested in annual meetings and occasional calls as needed. I did have several clients who had moved away but retained us as their advisor, however most of these clients were content with online or phone meetings or visiting us when they were in town.

Client Service Requirements: Investing

x	looking for help with investment strategy and selection
	looking for help implementing predetermined strategy
	desire for someone to bounce stock pick ideas off
	desire to choose and hold their own investment ideas
	wants to be involved in selection of specific investments
	desire to time the markets
	desire for the latest, newest investment product
	desire sophisticated investment ideas (derivatives, etc.)
	interested in complex details of recommendations
x	prefer simplified description of recommendations
x	ability to be patient with volatile markets
x	online monthly/quarterly statements
x	customized package of tax slips, etc. for investments

On occasion, I would meet experienced investors with a predetermined approach to investing. I found that if a client already has a set idea as to how to invest, the approach needed to be very similar to mine or the relationship could not survive. Some advisors relate better to the client who is interested in all of the details of an investment, others relate better to those clients who have no interest in investments but know they need to invest wisely to reach their goals. Some clients need to feel that they are smarter than and doing better than their peers. These clients usually want to hear about the "latest, greatest" investment idea and are very disappointed if they did not partake in the latest, apparently successful, trend. Over the years I came to accept that I was not very compatible with those people, largely because I was uncomfortable with the unknowns relating to new investment types and how the investment might react to the market and events. Eventually, incompatible clients would go to another advisor on their own accord or at my suggestion.

Our sustainable, compatible clients usually came to us recognizing their need for help with their strategy and selection of investments regardless of their personal success in very demanding professions. They appreciated our simplified explanations that backed up our recommendations and our openness to any and all questions. For example, a senior partner of a large accounting firm told me he appreciated our "willingness to answer dumb questions". Although frankly, I don't think that client ever asked any "dumb" questions.

Client Service Requirements: Financial Planning

x	prepare financial plan
x	financial plan year by year forecasting
	budgeting assistance
x	help in setting reasonable short- and long-term goals
x	retirement planning
x	protection planning (insurance)
x	estate planning
x	communicate with estate lawyer
x	charitable giving
x	financial planning for small business
	disabled person strategies

The term "Financial Plan" means different services to different people. It is important that the advisor understands the client's expectations to determine compatibility.

Client Service Requirements: Tax

	tax return preparation services
x	communicate with tax accountants
x	advice on tax strategies

I never prepared tax returns for clients (regardless of my accounting designation); however, I did communicate with clients' tax accountants at tax time in addition to confirming tax implications of my recommendations throughout the year. I would also suggest tax efficient investments and other tax saving strategies, such as those listed in the "Tax Return Services" and "Tax Strategies" checklists shown in the advisor's unique service model portion of this handbook.

Client service requirements can change over time. By the time I retired, most of my clients did not want to be involved with the day-to-day investment decisions and did not want to follow individual investments themselves. They did want the peace of mind of knowing that they understood the investment strategy and that a financial plan was in place, all in keeping with their goals and priorities. They appreciated their annual reviews and knew they would be contacted when necessary.

Client's Comfort and Preferences Regarding Payment for Advice and Service

These days, there are many different approaches to charging clients for the financial services they receive. The purpose of this checklist is to identify the methods the advisor is willing to employ with their clients. Some advisors will use different approaches with different clients based on the client's needs and what the clients are comfortable with. Other advisors offer only one approach to payment for advice and services. Those advisors will consider clients who don't accept that approach to be incompatible.

Client's Comfort/Preference Re Payment for Advice & Service

x	appreciate the benefits of the advice and services offered
x	comfort with transaction commissions
x	comfort with fees based on asset values
	comfort with hourly rate
	comfort with flat fee for service (e.g. X$ per financial plan)
x	comfort with fees embedded in products (funds, GICs, etc.)
x	will the client benefit enough to justify the costs of advice

I believe the advisor's approach to fees should be explained early in the relationship, probably soon after explaining the services offered and hopefully before the client asks. Particular attention should be paid to the explanation of embedded fees and commissions relating to mutual funds, new issues, bonds, GICs, etc. A lack of transparency regarding a client's fees and costs can do serious damage to a relationship based on trust. If a prospective client is not willing to pay for advice and services, the advisor is better off knowing before they invest a lot of time and resources pursuing the prospect.

I will discuss approaches to fees more thoroughly in the upcoming section "Component 5: Pricing and Client Cost Model". I expect to discuss how I converted clients from a transaction commission approach to fees based on asset values in my future handbook about processes and presentations.

Profitability: Immediate and Potential
An advisor's ability to relate to a potential client is not enough. The individual needs to have enough investable assets to benefit from the advice and to pay the advisor enough to justify the time and effort of the advisor and their team, or the relationship will not be mutually beneficial and therefore not sustainable. This checklist helps an advisor fill in their own criteria (minimums, ranges, etc.) to identify client relationships with enough potential profitability to pursue.

Profitability: Immediate and Potential

x	household annual revenue from client exceeds: _$2,000_
x	household investable assets exceed: _$500,000_
	client's current income exceeds: _____
	income growth potential
	potential inheritance
	source of quality referrals
x	member of profitable household

Potential (long-term) profitability is more important to advisors in the beginning and prime years of their career as they look to build a clientele to work with for many years.

Create a Summary of Your Practice's Compatible Groups and Criteria for Sustainable Clientele

Summarizing the results of your completed compatible and sustainable client checklists will identify who you want for clients and who you relate well with. This need not be a narrow definition. I related well with successful executives as well as their 80-year-old mother or father. You might have the personality and service model that is compatible with many. You will likely grow and evolve throughout your career becoming more compatible with some people and less compatible with others over time.

The following screen shot is the printable listing of all the items I checked on the previous sample checklists relating to identifying a compatible, sustainable clientele including a section for my comment(s). You can create a similar summary for your practice by running the "create summary" macro provided on the summary tab of the "Compatible Groups and Criteria for Sustainable Relationships" checklist template found in the business model checklists available on my website. The download will also include the sample.

C Timms Sample (Advisor Name)
Summary: Compatible Groups and Criteria for Sustainable Relationships
Date

IDENTIFY COMPATIBLE/TARGET GROUPS

Professions/Occupations

x	business executives
x	lawyers
x	accountants
2 or 3	architects
< 10	engineers

Business Owners and Organizations

x	any type of small business
x	charitable foundations
x	proprietorships
x	medical professional corporations
x	trusts
x	holding companies

Background/Social Groups

x	small town
x	big city

Common Interests

x	sports: _tennis_
x	vacation property: _cottage_

Age Group

x	middle age
x	approaching retirement
> 30%	early retirement
> 20%	RRIF age 72+

Family Experiences

x	single
x	married

Family Experiences (continued)

x	widowed
x	big family
x	small family (only child)
x	caring for children
x	caring for the elderly

Gender

x	women

CRITERIA FOR SUSTAINABLE INDIVIDUAL RELATIONSHIPS

Personality Traits

x	introvert
x	optimist
x	humble/modest
x	confident
x	collaborative
x	appreciates long-term relationships
x	delegator
x	thankful
x	patient
x	moderate risk taker
x	conservative
x	ultra-conservative
x	long-term focus

Client Goals

x	protect family from loss of life/income
x	financial independence
x	retire comfortably
x	liquidity/access to capital
x	leave a legacy (heirs or charity)
x	long-term gains expected range of returns: _6% - 10%_
x	fixed inc. expected return: _current 5yr GIC/gov't bond rates_
x	save for personal use real estate properties
x	maintain personal use real estate properties
x	plan for event (wedding or religious event)

Client Goals (continued)

x	spending/distributing wealth during lifetime
x	charitable giving during lifetime
x	train/teach their children
x	minimize tax
x	protect small business (personnel loss, marriage breakdown)

Client Service Requirements: Communication

x	accessible by phone
x	voicemail: _live person answers during office hours_
x	accessible by e-mail
x	review meeting, advisor's office frequency: _annual_
x	review meeting, client's home/office frequency: _occasional_
x	out-of-town review meetings: _North Ontario town_
x	minimum contact frequency: _annually_
x	maximum contact frequency: _weekly_
x	save/minimize client time requirements
x	written registered plan contribution reminders: _mail/e-mail_
x	call for registered plan contribution reminders

Client Service Requirements: Investing

x	looking for help with investment strategy and selection
x	prefer simplified description of recommendations
x	ability to be patient with volatile markets
x	online monthly/quarterly statements
x	customized package of tax slips, etc. for investments

Client Service Requirements: Financial Planning

x	prepare financial plan
x	financial plan year by year forecasting
x	help in setting reasonable short- and long-term goals
x	retirement planning
x	protection planning (insurance)
x	estate planning
x	communicate with estate lawyer
x	charitable giving
x	financial planning for small business

Client Service Requirements: Tax

x	communicate with tax accountants
x	advice on tax strategies

Client's Comfort/Preference Re Payment for Advice & Service

x	appreciate the benefits of the advice and services offered
x	comfort with transaction commissions
x	comfort with fees based on asset values
x	comfort with fees embedded in products (funds, GICs, etc.)
x	will the client benefit enough to justify the costs of advice

Profitability: Immediate and Potential

x	household annual revenue from client exceeds: _$2,000_
x	household investable assets exceed: _$500,000_
x	member of profitable household

COMMENTS

I have converted 80% of my clients to fee-based, likely 10% more to do.
I have converted about 50% of clients to discretionary.

It took me years to learn that if you feel like you are constantly bending over backwards to keep a client, you are probably not compatible and are fighting a losing battle. Let them go! You will both be happier. Hopefully, advisors using this checklist process will be able to identify their incompatible prospects and clients sooner than I did.

At the end of my career, my clients had a lot in common with each other and with me. We might not have agreed on absolutely everything (it is probably best not to discuss politics or religion), but they had goals and priorities I could relate to, most of which led to peace of mind for both the clients and myself. They were comfortable with my approach to investing, financial planning and overall service. They were appreciative and respectful of the time and effort of my team members and myself, and they were most comfortable with win-win relationships. Overall, I would say we had similar moral compasses and the same definition of smart. They were a pleasure for me to work with.

Relationships that satisfy many of your checklist items should be sustainable, win-win relationships. Ultimately, you will keep the clients that are most compatible with you, and you will be working to replace those that aren't. The more compatible you are with your client, the stronger the relationship. The stronger your relationship with a client, the more likely they will take all your advice and send you referrals. Clients will stay with you because you "get" them, and they will be your best source of new compatible clients. Your practice will be more focused, more efficient and more enjoyable for you.

"Appendix A: Why Advisors are Not Interchangeable" discusses, in more detail, why clients prefer to work with the same financial advisor for many years.

I intend to show how to convert the prospects into clients and serve existing clients through meetings, presentations, letters, etc. in a future handbook for financial advisors about processes and presentations.

Component 2: Unique Client Service Model

In today's world, the advisor's service model needs to go well beyond "robo-advisors" or discount investment service providers in order to compete. I expect that most robo-advisor and discount services are designed to meet the basic needs of the "average" client. A full-service advisor should "exceed the need" in every aspect of their practice to create loyal and appreciative clients. The service needs to be humanized and personal, recognizing each client's uniqueness, yet the service should be efficient and scalable. Clients need to feel they are receiving value for the fees and/or commissions paid. An advisor's efforts need to be visible so the clients can recognize the services they are receiving and, therefore, appreciate the effort and how they are benefiting.

I received the following note from a client when I retired.

> *"In wishing you the best, we want to thank you and your team for looking after our investments so well over the last 20 years. With a high level of professionalism, you have guided us through good times and bad with the consistent proven good advice to 'stay the course'. Throughout, you have communicated openly, proactively and reviewed and reported on our circumstances consistently. Not only did you provide guidance with our investment portfolio but also took the time to advise us in the overlapping areas of tax issues, insurance benefits, estate planning and will preparation. Lastly our yearly reviews were not only extremely helpful but cemented the personal relationships. Thank you!"*
>
> *—retired couple*

Clearly, the many services I offered mattered a great deal to the client. It is interesting to note that investment returns were not mentioned; however, communication was highlighted. The individual services are important, but how they are communicated goes a long way to ensure that the client benefits from and recognizes the value of the advisor and the service. An advisor can control service but can't control returns. A client's patience with returns is often the product of the trust earned by an advisor's clear and valuable communications.

This book is intended to help you identify what services you wish to offer. I intend to write another book in this series to give advice on processes and examples of how to provide those services including customizable presentations, reports, meeting agendas, letters, calculators, templates, etc. that will also be available on my website.

An advisor's challenge is to maximize the quality of service to their compatible, sustainable clients while operating a profitable practice. Much of this is accomplished by designing the service component of their business model to include services that are easily performed through efficient, largely delegable processes that will maximize the amount and quality of the advisor's time with clients.

Many advisors segment their clients into several groups based on revenue and assets under management often referred to as A, B, C or D clients. They will likely have different service models for the different segments. Advisors doing so will find the service model checklists helpful for identifying the services they wish to offer to each group of clients. I have more thoughts and ideas regarding segmenting clients near the end of this book including an additional checklist tool to facilitate the segmentation of an advisor's clientele.

When I started in the business with Merrill Lynch Canada in 1983, the term financial advisor was rarely, if ever, used. We were mostly stockbrokers who created portfolios of primarily individual stocks and bonds. Most contacts with clients involved buy/sell recommendations and providing information regarding various investments (research, price quotes and history, etc.). Unlike today, there were very few independent managed money choices available: only a small number of mutual funds and no separately managed accounts. The inclusion of in-depth financial planning was not prevalent until years later. Although many clients continued to need "stockbroker" services, I believe that much of my success as a financial advisor, and ability to attract clients, came from evolving to offer much more to satisfy my clients' goals and service requirements. Eventually, the services I offered matched the needs of the clients I was most compatible with because I came to understand who my compatible clients were and gained a further understanding of the services I should offer them. Knowing these two things allowed me to focus my learning, refine my processes and improve my practice management, resulting in the simultaneous serving of my clients' needs and growth of my practice. The more I articulated my service model, the easier it was for my team and me to market our services and to maintain the discipline necessary to focus our daily work on our priorities.

Attributes of a Successful Service Model

As I look back at the evolution of my business model and remember hearing about the services offered by other successful advisors, I have identified several overall service model attributes that add to an advisor's success. As you progress through the various checklists, I recommend keeping these attributes in mind.

Services Match Compatible, Sustainable Clientele Requirements

An advisor's selection of services to offer should match up with the services required by the clients the advisor has identified through the previously discussed compatible, sustainable clientele checklist. If the advisor's compatible, sustainable clients want/need a particular service, the advisor should consider offering it. The more clients who want a particular service, the more time and resources the advisor can afford to invest in the pursuit of the knowledge and the development of processes (presentations, templates, macros, calculators, etc.) needed to provide that particular service efficiently and effectively at minimum cost per client.

Narrows the Advisor's Focus
Advisors who are trying to be all things to all people inevitably spread themselves too thin and fail to be really good at anything. A good service model narrows the advisor's focus by identifying and concentrating on the services worth providing and eliminating the services deemed unnecessary or unappreciated by most of their clientele. The advisor and their team can focus their learning and their processes on the topics most relevant to the services they wish to offer. A well-thought-out and written service model will help facilitate the discipline of consistent actions and follow through.

Visibility of Advisor and Team Effort and Expertise
Obnoxious TV commercials and advertisements that belittle full-service advisors have made it more important than ever to show your clients what is being done for them, in addition to the time spent directly with them in meetings or phone calls. The services you offer should include evidence of behind the scenes expertise and effort. For example, if you have spent time meeting or listening to a money manager of a mutual fund that your clients hold, sending an e-mail/letter to the clients summarizing the meeting shows the clients that you are working for them in ways they could not do themselves. They won't know what you have done for them if you don't tell or show them!

Services Must be Reliable, Timely and Accurate Before Being Offered to All Clients

Good advisors don't offer services until they have developed their knowledge and processes enough to ensure the service will be timely and accurate. In other words, don't make promises until you are sure you can keep them. Consider testing new service ideas on a very small number of clients who are happy to be your test subjects before you introduce and promote the service to prospects and the rest of your clientele. For example, we tested some changes and additions to the presentations of our financial plans with various clients who requested modifications for themselves that we thought would be welcomed by many other clients. These clients were very appreciative and patient with our development process.

Affordable for Clients and Advisor

Affordability is a two-way street. The client needs to be able to afford to pay for your services, and you need to be able to afford the resources required to provide the services. This is ultimately a question of compatibility. A good advisor is always looking for more efficient/cheaper methods and processes to offer existing and additional services.

Scalable to Many Clients

The delivery of the services offered should be scalable to a large enough portion of an advisor's clientele to justify the work necessary to ensure quality and sustainability. A scalable service model lends itself to efficient processes and easy delegation. Before deciding that a service should be offered to clients and/or prospects, an advisor should determine if there are processes, templates, macros or calculators already developed and available through their firm or other services, such as my website, that the advisor can use and/or customize to deliver the service to many of their clients without much additional effort per client.

Repeatable to the Same Client

If you have provided the service once, you are setting a precedent that a client will likely expect you to repeat. Don't start something that you can't continue or make sure the client knows the particular service is a one-time event.

Advisor Enjoys Their Time at Work

An advisor's service model should allow the advisor to enjoy what they are doing most of the time. An advisor needs to think about what makes them happy at work and look to offer services that they enjoy providing and learning about. You may determine that today's environment requires some services for clients that you don't personally enjoy doing. Consider including these items in your service model along with a way to outsource or delegate enough of the service to your team so that you can still enjoy your time at work.

Background Work for Services Easily Delegated or Outsourced

Most successful advisors can delegate much of the work behind providing their selected services to team members or outsource within or outside their firm. As a practice grows, the advisor has less time to do the background work as they spend a higher percentage of their time in front of or in conversation with clients/prospects and performing activities best suited to their experience and expertise. A well-articulated service model will facilitate delegation to team members. I discuss delegating and outsourcing in greater detail in the *Team Building for Financial Advisors* handbook of this series.

Advisor is Proud of Their Service

Confidence and conviction are contagious. The more you believe in your services, the more team members, clients and prospects will believe in you and what you do. Successful advisors select services/products that they can provide with pride and confidence knowing that they are helping their clients.

Fosters Strong Relationships with Clients

Clients trust advisors who have proven themselves to be accessible, knowledgeable, attentive and responsive through the implementation of a well-thought-out service model that emphasizes communication. They will automatically think of contacting you with any financial question and/or when a life-changing event occurs. If you don't provide a service they need, they will still look to you for overall guidance and interaction with the professionals (accountants and/or lawyers) they have hired to perform those services. You will be their quarterback.

Flexible, Evolving

Successful advisors are always listening to industry news and clients for clues on how to improve existing services or develop new services. Good service models are easily modified to keep up with ever changing competition and client demands.

Major Categories of an Advisor's Unique Service Model

Although business models are unique to the individual advisor, there are many common challenges that all advisors face. Every advisor needs to allocate their resources to activities and services that will help their practice the most. There is an overwhelming number of potential services and products that an advisor must choose between. Before offering a service, an advisor must be confident that they have the time, skill and resources available to do so consistently, reliably, accurately and within a reasonable timeframe. In order to maximize their competitiveness, an advisor must be as smart, effective and efficient as possible in the selection and delivery of the services they offer. To simplify an advisor's selection of services/products to offer within their unique service model, I have divided services into four major categories and provided checklists for each.

Four Major Categories of Financial Advice Services

a. Client communication

b. Investing

c. Financial planning

d. Tax strategies and return preparation

The checklists for each of these categories provide a framework or structure for the choices that need to be made. Once again, I believe my checklists are fairly comprehensive but encourage advisors to add services or products that I have not included to their personal checklist (created from the template from my website). Note that the checklists also give you the opportunity to show who performs the service: you and your team, outsourced inside your firm, outsourced outside your firm. I have grouped the advisor and the team together for these checklists. I have also developed a duty allocation spreadsheet in the Appendix of the *Team Building for Financial Advisors* handbook to help advisors—with any team size—distribute duties amongst their team members. The advisor's delegation choices will depend on the skills and experience of their team members as well as the size of their clientele and will change as the team evolves through growth and/or turnover.

Client Communication Service Model

> *"Your clients want human contact because they seek collaboration, congruency, clarity, and communications. These are elements not provided by robo-advisors or discount brokers. At the end of the day, the reason they hire YOU is YOU—your humanity, the trust they have in you, and the comfort you provide especially when markets get sketchy."*
>
> —Craig Cmiel & David Leo
> (page 31 of *The Financial Advisor's Success Manual*) Kindle edition of December 2017 book

The comment below from a client of mine confirms the above statement.

> *"The world is too impersonal. I like that when I phone your office, you know me and my situation immediately versus all of the phone centers that companies use today. I did not have to go through numerous steps of phone menus.... Everyone has a 'know your client' form or information but you and your team really know the client."*
>
> —a client of over 20 years

Communication is the most critical of all the service model categories because the success of the other services depends on the success of the client communication model. Successful communication builds the trusting relationship necessary for the client to desire, accept and follow the advisor's advice regarding investments, financial planning, etc. The methods of client communication should demonstrate the client's importance to the advisor and that the advisor sees them as a unique individual with unique goals and aspirations. The communications should show that the advisor is working hard to identify and provide the particular services and advice appropriate for that client. The relationship resulting from good communication services prevents clients from going elsewhere for services you can provide and encourages them to contact you when any financial question arises and/or when a significant life-changing event occurs.

I have created a checklist with three sections to help advisors identify communication services they wish to offer to clients.

1. Client Contact Methods
2. Client Reminders
3. Personal Touches

The checklists allow you to clarify how many clients you provide the service for in the column of the service provider and dedicates a column for your description of the frequency of the service.

I intend to write another handbook in this series to give advice and examples of customizable presentations, reports, meeting agendas, letters, templates, etc. to assist advisors with client communications (also available on my website). Please note that additional client contact methods are included in this handbook's investing and financial planning service category sections, where appropriate (reports, financial plans, etc.).

Client Contact Methods

> *"The top reasons why high-net-worth clients leave their advisors are a failure to return a phone call in a timely manner, a failure to provide advice or ideas, and a failure to proactively contact the client," according to Vanguard Canada research.*
>
> — Michelle Schriver
> Investmentexecutive.com May 2, 2019

I saw this for myself when one of my clients told me he was bringing the money he had invested with an advisor at another institution to my group because "although they achieved a better return, I can't put up with the lack of accessibility of the advisor and her inadequate support".

It is important to understand the contact method and frequency an individual client prefers and act accordingly. We found that individual clients have different preferences regarding frequency of contact. A few clients were very clear that they preferred very little contact. A good contact management system will provide timely reminders for calling each individual client according to their specific wishes.

I think a service model should vary slightly with discretionary and non-discretionary clients. Advisors will need to be careful to ensure that transactional clients who hold only mutual funds and separately managed funds and clients whose accounts are completely discretionary are not neglected because calls are not triggered by trades, maturities or other transactions.

Client Contact Methods	You and Your Team	Outsource	Frequency
personal phone calls with updates	x		as needed
personal phone calls re transactions	x		as needed
voicemail for incoming calls	x		after hours
personal e-mail	x		as needed
face-to-face review at advisor's office	x		annually
face-to-face review at client's location	x		as needed
online review	x		as needed
mailout/e-mail review	x		as needed
market update letters/e-mails	mass blast		quarterly
money manager update letters/e-mails	specific group		as needed
stock update letters/e-mails	specific group		as needed
newsletters			
host seminars			
client focus groups			
website postings			
blogs			
videos			
podcasts			
social media			

(Service Performer spans the "You and Your Team" and "Outsource" columns)

Phone Calls Versus E-mails

Today's business world is relying more and more on communications by e-mail. I agree that in most cases e-mails are very efficient for the dissemination of accurate, timely information and provide useful notes of the interaction. However, even personalized e-mails can lack the human element that clients need to feel comfortable and to continue to choose you over the robo-advisors and discount competition. We would often send the information in writing and follow up with a phone call to discuss the content and engage the client, especially for important issues. The tone of vocal exchanges often results in better communication and a deeper relationship. Phone calls usually include more of the "how are you" and "what is going on in your life" conversations that are crucial in maintaining a strong relationship with clients. I recommend taking care to ensure some voice contact is maintained, especially if the client is not having face-to-face meetings.

Voicemail

> *"Your awareness of your client's needs is reflected in your providing a human response to telephone inquiries and ensuring that all calls are returned promptly. For this you are to be applauded. With other calls I make, when I hear the machine say 'your call is important to us' etc., I often wonder why in hell they don't answer the phone, if my call is so important to them."*
> —quote from a client's thank you letter

Many clients of the financial industry are greeted with voicemail for a high percentage of their calls to their financial service providers. I believe that the use of voicemail reduces the feeling of human contact and makes clients think they are not important enough for you to answer the phone. They may even picture you seeing their name and deciding not to answer! I think that all calls should be answered by a human whenever possible. In the long run, I think it is much more efficient and less frustrating for all involved. Phone tag is a frustrating time-waster for both the client and the advisor. Many of my clients mentioned their appreciation that a real, live person always answered the phone when they called my office during business hours.

If you must use voicemail, I recommend the use of a very engaging, friendly message. The voicemail should not make promises that you can't be sure of keeping. What do you gain by promising to return the call within one business day? You still have not spoken to the client, and now you have given them a reason to be even more frustrated if you don't return the call soon enough.

Face-to-Face Meetings

I am a big believer in face-to-face meetings. These meetings are the best opportunity to see and hear the client's hopes and fears. They give the advisor a chance to discover and discuss any doubts the client may have about past recommendations, current changes to their lives and their chances of achieving their goals. As previously stated in a quote by one of my clients, these review meetings "cemented the personal relationships". Nothing beats seeing a person's face to judge how they really feel. I recommend one in-person review meeting per year and maybe more in the early stages of a relationship. At the beginning of a relationship and during every meeting, we would ask a client how often they wanted to meet. We would suggest a minimum of once a year. We would also suggest meeting if the client showed signs of nervousness about their investments (most likely during a bear market) or experienced a significant change or event in their life. The agenda for these meetings will be discussed in detail in my future handbook about processes and presentations, and the templates for the agendas will be made available on my website.

Online Meetings

We used "GoToMeeting" for online meetings with clients who preferred not to travel to our office, sometimes conferencing in family members or professionals in different locations. We found sharing our screen with clients very useful when discussing our review agenda and for pointing out items on reports or spreadsheets. We did not use cameras because I thought it would add to technical complications and because it was difficult to maintain proper eye contact. I preferred real eye contact and the shaking of hands; however, an online meeting was far better than no meeting at all.

Mailout/E-mail Reviews

Over the course of my career, we would sometimes use mailout or e-mail reviews when a client was unable to meet in person. The presentations for these reviews were very similar to a regular face-to-face meeting. We would always follow up with a phone call to see if the client had any questions or concerns after they had time to review the material.

Written Updates re Companies/Stocks and Money Managers

These written updates show the client that the advisor is working for them behind the scenes, following particular investments and doing research the client is likely unable or unwilling to do. Our updates included references to our recent conversations with individual money managers, reminding clients why we used that manager and usually confirming our confidence in them. Many clients have told me that these updates helped them relax knowing that my team and I were on top of their investments.

Websites, Blogs, Videos and Podcasts

I think every advisor should have a website. A website should be the equivalent of a detailed, personalized marketing brochure easily referred to by clients and prospects. The website can facilitate the use of blogs, videos, podcasts, etc., all of which can be used to highlight your unique service model. I will go into websites in greater detail in my handbook on processes and presentations.

Social Media

I would use social media with caution. Be very careful to protect the identity of your clients. You don't want to be inadvertently supplying your client contact list to the competition. Be sure that your firm has approved the use and that you take advantage of any advice and training the firm provides. As social media is still a relatively new form of business communication, there is likely a lot of issues that we don't know about yet, similar to the risks of brand-new investment products. Try to minimize the distractions provided by social media by switching off alerts and notifications. Minimize the amount of updating required, possibly by linking references of you on the various social media sites to your website so you only have to update the one location.

Speed of Response

The speed of your response to clients is critical. Regardless of the method of communication, your response time to a client enquiry is very important. A quick response time shows that you value the relationship and respect the client's wishes even when the request might seem trivial to you and your team. One client told us that our "speed of response exceeded what is needed", and he was impressed when he wrote an e-mail on a Sunday night and had a response from us the next morning.

Client Reminders

Client reminders are one more way to build trust and outperform your competition, especially robo-advisors and discount service providers. If a client knows they can count on you and your team to remind them whenever action is required, they can truly relax, knowing that you are taking care of them and nothing will fall through the cracks.

| | Service Performer | | |
Client Reminders	You and Your Team	Outsource	Frequency
maturing GICs, CSBs, bonds, etc.	x		as needed
RRSP contributions	x		annually
TFSA contributions	x		annually
RESP contributions	x		annually
life insurance premium reminders	x		annually
disability insurance premium reminders	x		annually
critical illness premium reminders	x		annually
RRSP conversion to RRIF/annuity	x		annually
LIRA conversion to LRIF/annuity	x		annually
tax loss selling	x		annually

My team and I reminded clients about contributions to registered accounts initially with semi-personalized, written reminders including standard paragraphs and return envelopes. More recently, we would also provide the instructions for e-transfers. The easier it is for a client to contribute, the more likely the advisor will receive the contribution. We only sent the reminders to clients who had the relevant type of account and who had not already made their maximum contribution. We would follow up the mailout with a phone call a week or so later. For registered accounts where a late contribution could cost the client a tax deduction (RRSP) or a credit (RESP), our calls would persist until the contribution was made or clearly decided against. Many clients have told us they appreciated those reminders, especially when they were very busy with their careers and families. Templates for these reminders will be available on my website and in my future handbook regarding processes and presentations for clients and prospects.

We would call clients to remind them of the GICs, bonds, etc. maturing not only with us but also those maturing at other institutions. Clients have been known to forget they have Canada Savings Bonds that unfortunately stop paying interest after their maturity date. Of course, these reminders helped the client, but also gave us the opportunity to suggest that they consolidate more of their investments with us.

Personal Touches

Sincere personal touches usually go above and beyond what robo-advisors, discount services and even full-service competitors are willing to provide. They show your humanity and are an indication that you think and care about your clients as unique individuals. Keep in mind that some personal touches might set a precedent that a client will expect you to repeat: you should not start something you will be unable or unwilling to continue (for example, giving event tickets to clients). Listen for clues to what they enjoy and, where possible, tailor your gift to the individual. Gifts are best when they are an indication that you have been listening to the client.

Personal Touches	Service Performer		Frequency
	You and Your Team	Outsource	
holiday season cards	every client		annually
team picture	every client	photos	annually
family picture	10 clients		annually
holiday season gifts/donations	some clients	x	annually
sympathy cards/gifts	x		as needed
personal celebration gifts	rarely		special events
birthday cards/letters			
birthday calls			
sports/entertainment tickets	rarely		special events
individual client lunches/dinners	rarely		special events
individual client entertainment events	rarely		special events
book gifts	x		sometimes
referral thank-you calls	x		all referrals
referral thank-you gifts	x		sometimes

Holiday Cards:
I highly recommend sending holiday cards that include a picture of the advisor and the team. My clients really appreciated holiday season team picture cards. Eventually, the picture and all of our signatures became the card itself. Some clients told me that they put our picture card on their desk or refrigerator, so they could see the face of the person they were talking to when they called my office.

Holiday Gifts:
Early in my career, I started sending food gift baskets to celebrate the holiday season. Over the years I learned that some clients really appreciated the baskets (especially older widows) while others asked me to replace the basket with a donation to their favorite charities, some preferred golf balls while still others told me I should not bother at all!

Sympathy Cards/Gifts:

I think a modest expression of sympathy with a thoughtful note during a client's time of loss lets the client know that you are thinking of them without intruding. Sometimes a small gift of flowers or a food basket or a donation to a charity suggested by the obituary is appropriate.

Birthday Letters:

In the early years of my career, we sent out birthday letters to clients. In time, I realized that so many institutions were sending birthday cards that clients began to feel the birthday wishes were overly automated and an insincere indication of "pretending to care". I know one successful advisor who is committed to calling his clients on their birthday every year. This is a big commitment that may be difficult to maintain, especially if the advisor has a large number of clients.

Book Gifts:

Several times during my career, I stumbled upon a book that I deemed appropriate for some or all of my clients. Some examples are listed below:

Investing
- *Shifting Gears: Thriving in the New Economy* by Nuala Beck

- *Simple Wealth, Inevitable Wealth* by Nick Murray

- *Debunkery: Learn It, Do It, and Profit from It—Seeing Through Wall Street's Money-Killing Myths* by Ken Fisher

Financial Planning
- *Raising Financially Fit Kids* by Joline Godfrey

- *The Healthy Business: Shape Up, Survive & Thrive* by Rosalyn J. Cronin, CMA

- *Get Inspired to Retire: Over 150 Ideas to Help Find Your Retirement* by David Saylor and Greg Heffington

- *101 Secrets for a Great Retirement: Practical, Inspirational & Fun Ideas for the Best Years of Your Life* by Mary Helen and Shuford Smith

Estate Planning
- *You Can't Take It with You: The Common-Sense Guide to Estate Planning for Canadians* by Sandra E. Foster

- *The Family Fight: Planning to Avoid It* by Barry Fish and Les Kotzer

- *Creating the Good Will: The Most Comprehensive Guide to Both the Financial and Emotional Sides of Passing on Your Legacy* by Elizabeth Arnold

Tax Strategies
- *Tax Planning for You and Your Family* by KPMG

I would sometimes give a book to all clients. Sometimes I would give a new or existing client a book as appropriate during a face-to-face appointment. The gift of a book is a little something extra that may help strengthen the relationship and may help to reinforce some of your views or recommendations.

Referral Thank You:
I highly recommend calling and maybe sending a modest gift to thank the source of a referral.

Create A Summary of Your Practice's Communication Services

Summarizing the results of your completed communication service model checklists will provide a list of the communication services you wish to offer clients.

The following screen shot is the printable listing of all of the items I checked on the sample checklists to identify my practice's client communication service model including space for my comments. The checklist template for creating a similar summary for yourself is included in the business model checklist template available on my website. The download will also include the sample.

C Timms Sample (Advisor Name)
Summary Of Service Model for Client Communication
Date

Client Contact Methods	Service Performer		
	You and Your Team	Outsource	Frequency
personal phone calls with updates	x		as needed
personal phone calls re transactions	x		as needed
voicemail for incoming calls	x		after hours
personal e-mail	x		as needed
face-to-face review at advisor's office	x		annually
face-to-face review at client's location	x		as needed
online review	x		as needed
mailout/e-mail review	x		as needed
market update letters/e-mails	mass blast		quarterly
money manager update letters/e-mails	specific group		as needed
stock update letters/e-mails	specific group		as needed

Client Reminders			
maturing GICs, CSBs, bonds, etc.	x		as needed
RRSP contributions	x		annually
TFSA contributions	x		annually
RESP contributions	x		annually
life insurance premium reminders	x		annually
disability insurance premium reminders	x		annually
critical illness premium reminders	x		annually
RRSP conversion to RRIF/annuity	x		annually
LIRA conversion to LRIF/annuity	x		annually
tax loss selling	x		annually

Personal Touches			
holiday season cards	every client		annually
team picture	every client	photos	annually
family picture	10 clients		annually
holiday season gifts/donations	some clients	x	annually
sympathy cards/gifts	x		as needed
personal celebration gifts	rarely		special events
sports/entertainment tickets	rarely		special events
individual client lunches/dinners	rarely		special events
individual client entertainment events	rarely		special events

Personal Touches (continued)

book gifts	x		sometimes
referral thank-you calls	x		all referrals
referral thank-you gifts	x		sometimes

Identifying the communication services you wish to offer should help you market your services, list the features you require in your contact management system and help you determine who on your team will perform each service item.

Methods of communication are constantly changing as technology evolves. I expect the communications checklists I have provided will change and grow dramatically with the passage of time. An advisor should seek to learn about and take advantage of new communications technology while understanding that human beings will always want to be heard, understood and responded to. Advisors should evaluate new technology based on its ability to help them hear, understand and respond to clients more effectively and efficiently. In the interests of minimizing duplication, I have included other very important client contact services in the following investing and financial planning service model checklists.

My future handbook on processes and presentations for clients and prospects will give advice regarding efficient processes and effective presentations, letters, reports, etc. including examples, templates and methods of communicating services to clients so that they understand and value the services they are receiving.

Investing Advice Service Model

"To invest successfully over a lifetime…. What's needed is a sound intellectual framework for making decisions and the ability to keep emotions from corroding that framework."

—Warren Buffet

An advisor's well-thought-out and clearly articulated investing advice service model should provide the intellectual framework and structure for determining the advisor's resulting product shelf. It will give the advisor the criteria needed for future investment decisions and improve the advisor's ability to keep emotions out of the decision-making process.

There are many different approaches to selecting investments for clients. An advisor must decide what approaches they are comfortable with and willing and able to offer to their clients. This is effectively selecting their own product shelf.

I believe that the investment service model of the most successful advisors will reflect their own comfort levels and interests, to the extent that their own personal and family investments will fall within the range of the overall advice, strategies and investment vehicles that they provide to their clients. Clients like to know that, where possible, an advisor has put their own money "where their mouth is", and the advisor's personal experiences will coincide with their own. It is also more efficient to be following your own investments while you are following your clients.

The following is a short history of how my approach to investing evolved to an investment advice service model that suited the comfort levels of both myself and my compatible, sustainable clientele.

For as long as I can remember, I have allocated a client's portfolio between safe investments and riskier investments (those for growth). My strategy for the safe/fixed income portion of clients' portfolios was relatively constant throughout my career relying largely on maturity ladders of government guaranteed securities and high credit rated preferred shares. Initially, for the growth/ equity component of a client's portfolio, I picked 15-25 stocks from companies traded on Canadian and American stock exchanges that looked well priced based on "growth at a reasonable price" (GARP) criteria and that were followed and favoured by my firm's research analysts. In my first two years in the business, I was also willing to experiment with some investments my clients suggested including stock and index options. (OEX index options were very popular at the time.) Although none of the clients "blew up", I quickly learned that I was not comfortable with the risks associated with speculating, even though it was considered "appropriate" for those clients. I also concluded that "the most successful investor is a patient investor", and my new priority became investing in a way that helped clients be patient with volatile stock markets. I developed my approach/service model for investing accordingly. Looking for less volatility through greater global and industry diversification, I gradually turned to managed money (mutual funds and separately managed accounts) with a variety of investment styles for the common equity portion of my clients' portfolios. I eventually stopped choosing individual common stocks for my clients.

My investment strategy and preferences evolved with my knowledge and experience, as well as the investment industry's evolving product lines. Eventually, my clientele reflected those preferences as well. As I grew in confidence and fine-tuned my approach to investing, I became more insistent that clients follow my best investment advice. About 20 years into my career, I found another advisor for the clients who were no longer compatible with the investment portion of my service model largely because they wished to continue to be involved in a common stock picking process.

Once I had narrowed down the strategies and securities that I would recommend and follow for my clients, my team and I could take the time to focus on in-depth research regarding those items and create more efficient processes. We were better able to describe and promote our investment services with confidence and conviction. I was also able to quickly explain to clients why a new potential investment they heard or read about did, or did not, fit our investment approach and whether it was suitable for their portfolio.

Developing and/or Articulating Your Approach to Investing

In order to develop your practice's investment strategy and product shelf, you need to understand the priorities of yourself and your long-term sustainable clientele. What do the clients want and need, and what will they be comfortable with? You already accomplished this if you created your personal Summary of Your Practice's Compatible Groups and Criteria for Sustainable Clientele, as described earlier in this book.

My sustainable clientele was comprised of moderate- to low-risk takers whose priorities were retiring comfortably, taking care of their family and sleeping at night. They were looking for financial peace of mind. In order to provide my clients and myself with peace of mind, my approach to investing needed to protect clients from the big mistake while still providing the opportunity for returns that would help them reach their goals. This meant minimizing overall volatility through diversification, investment selection and the use of strategies that did not involve leverage and were easily explained. I was also unwilling to accept high risk in any individual investment even if the low correlation with the rest of the portfolio would technically reduce overall risk. These basic principles remained constant throughout my career, while the application of those principles evolved with industry products and platforms.

The following investment service model checklists, decision flow chart and related discussions are provided to help advisors identify, describe and analyze the investment services and securities they wish to provide to clients:

- Overall Investment Advice Services Checklist
- Steps Toward Security Selection for Your Compatible, Sustainable Clients (create your product shelf)
- Investment Platforms
- Investment Account Types
- Investment Reporting
- Tax Reporting for Investments

The checklists include columns to indicate the service performer (advisor and/or team, outsourced within the firm, outsourced externally) and if those services can be provided on a discretionary basis. As an example, I marked the service items I provided during the last several years of my practice with an "x" or further detail. Some sections also include considerations for completing that section of the checklist and my personal insights into why my approach to investing was successful with my clientele. The checklist templates available through my website include spaces to add items that do not appear on these lists.

I recommend including team members in the checklist process as much as their experience and capabilities allow. In the later stages of my career, my team members, especially my associates, were very involved in all aspects of the investing service model. My team contributed to the selection of strategies and securities as well as the development of processes and presentations to apply our investment approach to our clients' portfolios.

All of the previously mentioned attributes of a successful service model are very applicable to investment services. I have listed them here for you to keep in mind as you progress through the items on your checklists:

- Services match compatible, sustainable clientele requirements
- Narrows the advisor's focus

- Visibility of advisor and team effort and expertise
- Services must be reliable, timely and accurate before offered to all clients
- Affordable for clients and advisor
- Scalable to many clients
- Repeatable to the same client
- Advisor enjoys their time at work
- Background work for services easily delegated or outsourced
- Advisor is proud of their service
- Fosters strong relationships with clients
- Flexible, evolving

Overall Investment Advice Services Checklist

The overall investment advice service checklist refers to general investment services. I would expect advisors to provide the first five services on the checklist to meet minimum industry standards. An advisor needs to determine a client's goals and educate them regarding the expected returns and volatility of various investment strategies and securities while helping the client assess their risk tolerances.

If an advisor's practice does not include the buying and selling of investments/specific securities for clients, they may wish to help clients complete these checklists to assist them in finding the appropriate individual or institution to select the specific securities and/or execute the transactions.

	Service Performer		
Overall Investment Advice Services	**You and Your Team**	**Outsource**	**Discretionary**
determine client's investment goals	x		x
educate: various strategies, securities, etc.	seminar		
educate: expectation of returns & volatility	seminar		
assess client risk tolerance	x		
summarize client financial position/details	x		

Overall Investment Advice Services (continued)

make asset class allocation decisions	flow chart		x
provide investment policy statement	x		x
implement (buy/sell investments)	x		x
consider tax effects of recommendations	x	consult acct	
year-end tax loss selling	x	consult acct	

Educating Clients

My approach and process for helping an individual client or prospect determine their financial goals and risk tolerances was set out in my meeting agendas. Early in my career, I developed a Power Point seminar titled "Investing for Peace of Mind with the Timms Financial Group" to educate clients during appointments. This seminar outlined my logic behind asset allocation, investment strategies, security selection and what to expect from different asset classes. The seminar was updated constantly throughout my career.

Educating our clients/prospects was always a big priority for us. We would explain the logic behind our approach to asset allocation, investment strategies and why we chose the specific individual securities for their portfolio. This education was provided through many of the communication methods previously mentioned (see "Client Contact Methods" checklist) in addition to portions of our Investing for Peace of Mind seminar. I believe that the relatively good investment returns that my clients enjoyed over the long term were a result of their patience with poor short-term returns caused by volatile markets. I believe that their patience was a direct result of the initial and ongoing education we provided to prepare people for market volatility. The education produced reasonable client expectations for both short- and long-term returns. During bear markets we would provide all clients with encouraging and relevant historical references proving that investors who were patient in the past were eventually rewarded. Overall, we provided the education we thought each individual client needed and/or desired to give them peace of mind and inspired the patience we believed was required to be a successful investor.

My clients' appreciation of my desire to educate and explain the logic behind recommendations in terms they easily understood was reflected in their comments when I asked them what they looked for in an advisor. Many clients told me that they appreciated how we "spoke plainly" or "spoke in layman's terms" or used "plain language". Many clients mentioned they liked our graphs and visual explanations shown during our "regular contact and portfolio reviews". One client said he liked how we "made complicated understandable". These comments came from very well-educated clients (lawyers, accountants and engineers) as well as less sophisticated clients.

The "Investing for Peace of Mind with the Timms Financial Group" seminar led to a list of questions for the client/prospect and I to answer together when determining the allocations and specific investments suitable for that client. This list of questions later evolved into my Investment Allocation Decision flowchart, as described in the next section. The seminar and the appointment agenda templates will be available through my website as modifiable templates along with Investment Policy Statement templates upon completion of my handbook on processes and presentations.

Investment Allocation Decision Flow Chart
An Investment Allocation Decision Flow Chart similar to my example shown below will serve as a concise and simplified summary of the advisor's approach to investing and a practical worksheet for meetings and conversations with clients regarding the allocations in their investment portfolio. An advisor will be more able to design their own Investment Allocation Decision Flow Chart after they have completed the "Steps Toward Security Selection for Your Compatible, Sustainable Clients" checklists discussed in the next section.

I developed the Investment Allocation Decision Flow Chart to help advisors work with their clients to logically progress through the questions that need to be answered while formulating the allocations within a client's portfolio. It will also provide the basis for the investment policy statement and the selection of investments for the client's portfolio.

I must admit that I did not convert my list of client investment allocation questions into this flow chart until after I retired. I had simply listed the allocation decisions in writing on my meeting agendas. I thought a flow chart would be a better presentation but never got around to designing it until I started working on these books.

I think the flow chart clearly and concisely portrays my overall approach to investing and the allocation decisions that needed to be made for each client's portfolio. The flow chart can serve as a worksheet for the advisor and the client to fill in together, ultimately providing the client and advisor with a record of the decisions and the overall plan for their investments. The flow chart can then be used by the advisor and their team to write the investment policy statement and formulate the course of action (selection of securities/products from the advisor's shelf). The sample flow chart (Power Point) is available on my website as a starting point for advisors.

Client Investment Allocation Decision Flow Chart (excluding cash reserves)

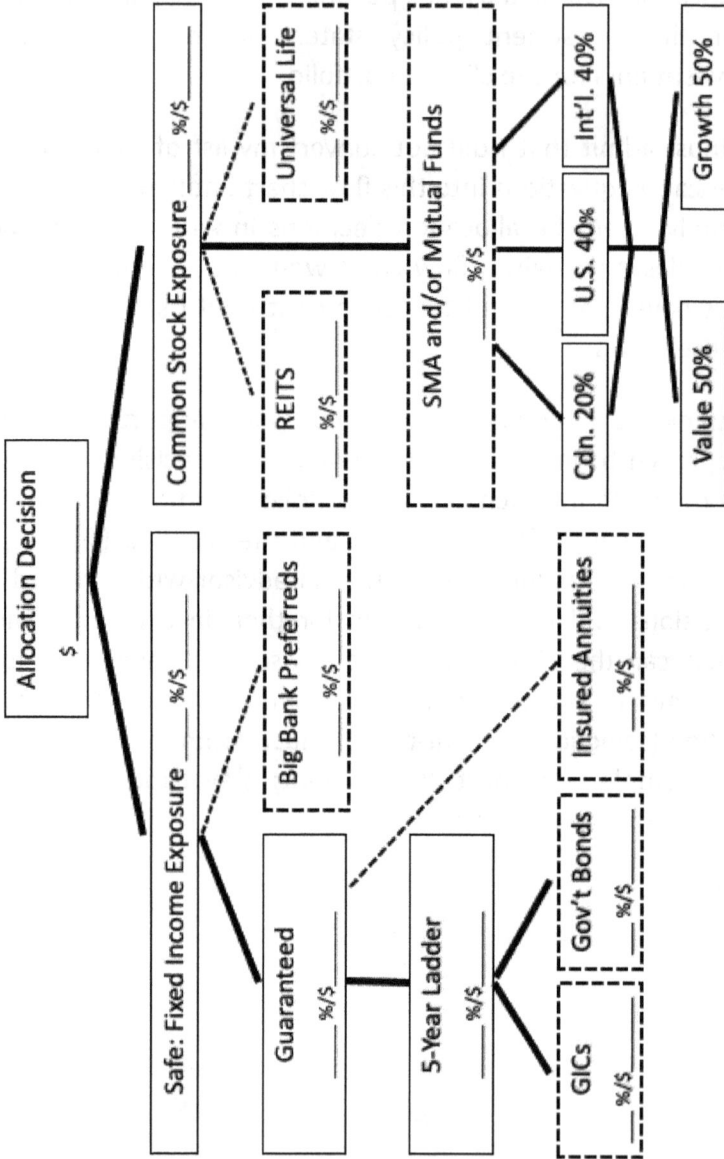

Allocation Decision
$ ____

Safe: Fixed Income Exposure ____ %/$

Common Stock Exposure ____ %/$

Big Bank Preferreds ____ %/$

Guaranteed ____ %/$

5-Year Ladder ____ %/$

GICs ____ %/$

Gov't Bonds ____ %/$

Insured Annuities ____ %/$

REITS ____ %/$

Universal Life ____ %/$

SMA and/or Mutual Funds ____ %/$

Cdn. 20%

U.S. 40%

Int'l. 40%

Value 50%

Growth 50%

Note that the flow chart is for investments not including cash reserved for emergencies or upcoming events. The solid lines on the flow charts lead to asset groups that were employed in most of our clients' portfolios, while the dotted lines refer to those asset groups that were appropriate for a smaller set of clients.

The boxes under SMAs and mutual funds reflect my ultimate goal of balance between countries and investment styles. The dotted boxes refer to sections of your product shelf—lists of individual securities/products that you would recommend or purchase for your clients' portfolio.

Tax Considerations
After the client's risk profile has been established and the investments asset class exposure, strategy and delivery vehicles have been determined, then the investments should be allocated to the appropriate types of account (Tax Free Savings Account (TFSA) vs retirement accounts vs corporate account, etc.) based on tax efficiency. For example, dividends are usually best outside of registered accounts so that they can receive the dividend tax credit. The "best" account types for particular investments need to be re-evaluated when tax rules and/or expected returns change.

Steps Toward Security Selection for Your Compatible, Sustainable Clients
The purpose of this section is to help advisors narrow down and simplify the investment decision process. Services, such as selecting asset class exposure security sets, investment strategies and investment delivery vehicles, are expanded upon in checklists on separate tabs of the same spreadsheet. It is impossible to list every possible asset class, strategy or delivery vehicle, so my website's checklist template provides space to add items and the ability to modify descriptions of listed items so each advisor can easily customize their investment service model.

There is a massive number of different potential investments for an independent financial advisor to choose for their clients. No one advisor can be expected to know everything about all of the investments available. You need to narrow the scope of potential selections. Every advisor needs to determine their own short, manageable product/investments shelf so they can be confident in their knowledge regarding each investment's potential risks, benefits and suitability before they recommend or buy them for their clients.

I think an advisor should be willing to explore a new investment (asset class, strategy, delivery vehicle or individual security) to see if it fits their compatible, sustainable clientele before eliminating or ignoring it. The criteria determined by articulating your investment advice service model should allow you or your team to analyze new investment ideas quickly and effectively, enabling you to give intelligent, well-thought-out answers when accepting or rejecting a popular new investment. This capability will add to an advisor's credibility, help an advisor discover appropriate new investments, assure clients they are not missing out and bolster the client's confidence in the advisor's overall advice.

An advisor should expect to modify their product/investment shelf as industry product choices evolve and the investments themselves change in value, etc.

I have developed a four-step process to help an advisor identify the contents of the investment securities/product shelf they are comfortable recommending to their clients. The steps are as follows:

1. Select Asset Class Exposure by Security Sets

2. Select Investment Strategies

3. Select Investment Delivery Vehicles

4. Choose Securities for Product Shelf

When you have completed the checklists for steps 1-3 it will be easier for your team and you to focus on investments that will be relevant to your sustainable clients and quickly eliminate potential investments based on your checklist. I intend to cover processes for step 4, choosing actual securities, in my next book in this series regarding processes and presentations for clients and prospects.

Once again, I have used the final years of my practice as an example. My selections reflect the conservative nature of myself and my compatible, sustainable clientele.

Asset Class Exposure Security Sets
Initially, an advisor must decide what sets of assets their clients should ultimately be exposed to, in order to reach their goals and stay within the comfort levels of the clients and the advisor. This checklist groups many sets of securities under the basic asset classes of Cash & Equivalents, Fixed Income, Common Equities and Alternatives.

| | Service Performer | | |
| | You and | | |
Cash & Equivalents Exposure	Your Team	Outsource	Discretionary
high interest savings accounts	x		x
T-bills	x		x
firms' cash management accounts	x		x
money market funds			
bank paper (banker's acceptance)			
commercial paper			

My selections under the cash & equivalents section reflect my belief that assets in this set need to be as safe as possible, usually with a government guarantee. Cash and cash equivalents were only used in my clients' portfolios to reserve funds for emergencies or a client's specific need for cash on a specific date, such as payments for a house/mortgage, tax installments, tuition, wedding, car purchase, etc.

| Fixed Income Exposure | Service Performer | | |
	You and Your Team	Outsource	Discretionary
GICs	x		x
gov't bonds: federal	x		x
gov't bonds: provincial	x		x
gov't bonds: municipal			
short-term (one to five years)	x		x
mid-term (six to ten years)			
long-term (over ten years)			
compounding bonds/strips	x		x
corporate bonds			
convertible bonds			
U.S. bonds	x		x
international bonds			
preferred shares	x		x
insured annuities	x	x	
mortgage-backed securities			
private mortgages			

I employed fixed income as the safe portion of clients' portfolios. As a result, I restricted my security sets to government or government guaranteed bonds and GICs plus big bank preferred shares and insured annuities. We reduced interest rate risk by limiting ourselves to fixed income securities maturing within less than six years. We also avoided currency risk by keeping fixed income investments in the currency that the client intended to ultimately spend. We often held U.S. bonds to provide income and currency protection for "snowbirds".

Common Equities Exposure	Service Performer		
	You and Your Team	Outsource	Discretionary
common stocks	x		x
all-cap	x		x
large-cap	x		x
mid-cap			
small-cap			
specific sector: _____			
Canadian	x		x
U.S.	x		x
international	x		x
emerging markets			
specific country/region: _____			

My unwillingness to accept high risk in any individual investment meant that our coverage of mid-cap and small-cap companies was achieved through our all-cap exposure and that our emerging markets coverage was achieved through our international equity exposure. Our exposure to all sectors was achieved by investing outside of Canada. Our global diversification reduced volatility during extremely volatile times, largely because the U.S. dollar rose as investors around the world moved to the U.S. dollar in times of extreme uncertainty, mitigating the losses of portfolios measured in Canadian dollars. This mitigation of losses occurred dramatically during the global financial crisis when the Canadian dollar fell by over 20% in relation to the U.S. dollar from the U.S. stock market peak in October 2007 to the market bottom in March 2009.

Alternatives Exposure	Service Performer		
	You and Your Team	Outsource	Discretionary
commercial real estate	x		x
residential rental real estate			
commodities: _____			
foreign currencies: _____			
cryptocurrencies: _____			
start-up companies			
private equities			

My lack of selections on the alternatives exposure list reflects my desire for liquidity, my lack of comfort with more volatile securities and my desire for identifiable long-term track records.

Investment Strategies

Your selection of strategies identifies how you will accomplish the exposure to the asset class security sets identified in the previous checklist. A well-diversified portfolio will likely include a combination of many investment strategies. Understanding which strategies you and your clients are not comfortable with will allow you to eliminate many new investment ideas quickly.

The passive maturity ladder provided the safety and lack of price volatility I was looking for in the fixed income side of the portfolio, allowing the client to be more patient with the equity side of their portfolio where some volatility was unavoidable. The combination of strategies I selected for equity exposure ensured diversification by industry, style and country, and once again reduced volatility.

| Investment Strategies | Service Performer | | |
	You and Your Team	Outsource	Discretionary
passive maturity ladder	x		x
passive fixed income (indexes)			
monthly income			
high-yield fixed income			
interest rate speculation			
passive equity (indexes)			
equity top-down by sector			
equity top-down by country			
equity bottom-up all sectors	x		x
equity bottom-up all countries	x		x
equity style growth	x		x
equity style value	x		x
equity style momentum			
equity style core			
equity style GARP	x		x
equity style high dividend			
socially responsible investing			
sustainable or ESG investing			

Investment Strategies (continued)

dollar cost averaging	x		
pre-authorized contributions	x		
rebalancing	x		x
covered call equity strategy			
borrowing to invest			
options strategy: _____			
currency hedging			
currency speculation			
selling short: _____			

I learned very early in my career that I was not interested in speculating in high-risk investments, especially those that could go to zero. This meant I quickly eliminated all investments and/ or strategies involving leverage (options, borrowing to invest, derivatives). I was also uncomfortable with currency and commodity speculation. I did not employ currency hedging strategies because I believed it would limit the diversification benefits provided by my non-Canadian investments.

Investment Delivery Vehicles/Securities

Once you have decided which asset class security sets you are comfortable exposing your clients to and the strategies you wish to employ, you need to choose the investment delivery vehicles from which to finally choose specific investments.

Advisors need to determine whether individual securities or a combination of collections of securities is best for the asset class exposure they wish to achieve with their investment strategies. Choosing individual securities usually gives the advisor more control over the exact amount and type of risk of the investment. Choosing collections of investments, such as mutual funds, ETFs, SMAs, etc., relinquishes some of that control, but usually provides a greater variety of securities than could be achieved by choosing individual securities. Some advisors may find that they wish to use individual securities for some asset classes and collections for other asset classes. For example, I used individual securities for fixed income and collections (mutual funds and SMAs) for common equity exposure.

Investment Delivery Vehicles	Service Performer		
	You and Your Team	Outsource	Discretionary
individual high interest savings accounts	x		x
individual t-bills	x		
money market funds			
commercial paper			
individual bonds: _fed and prov gov't_	x		x
individual GICs: _CDIC insured_	x		x
individual preferred shares: _big banks_	≥p2		
individual common stocks: _____			
initial public offerings: _preferreds_	x		x
ETFs bond indexes			
ETFs balanced indexes			
ETFs stock indexes			
ETFs managed			
ETFs: _____			
mutual funds bonds			
mutual funds balanced			
mutual funds stocks	x		x
mutual funds alternatives			
SMA* fixed income portfolios			
SMA* balanced portfolios			
SMA* equity portfolios	x	firm	x
SMA*: _____			
pools			
seg./guaranteed investment funds			
universal life			
insured annuities personal	x	firm	
insured annuities corporate	x	firm	
options, derivatives			
structured products (linked notes)			
futures			
hedge funds			
private equity			
limited partnerships: _____			
income trusts (including REITS)	x		x
tax assisted investments			
real estate property direct ownership			

* SMA = Separately Managed Accounts

Interest earning securities: I chose individual bonds and GICs for clients because I wanted the clients to own the maturity date so they knew exactly when their capital would be returned and exactly how much interest they would earn. I expected to hold all bonds and GICs to maturity. I restricted our selections to federal and provincial guaranteed bonds or GICs to eliminate the risk of loss of capital. As a result, I avoided mutual funds, SMA managers and ETFs for bonds. For the same reason, I also avoided "balanced" mutual funds, SMA managers and ETFs that contained bonds.

Insured annuities: We purchased insured annuities for individuals and private corporations with long-term capital that they did not need access to for the rest of the individual's life and wished to maximize their after-tax income while minimizing their estate tax.

Preferred shares: I restricted my preferred share choices to big bank preferreds that contained a feature that reduced exposure to changing interest rates (retractable, rate reset, floating rate). My product shelf of preferred shares varied greatly over the years as the industry invented new features and old features disappeared as older issues were redeemed.

Common equity: For the first 10 years or so of my career, I enjoyed the intellectual stimulation of picking stocks. I know many advisors where the stock selection process continues to be the most fun for them. Those advisors are also confident that their returns after fees compare well with those of money managers and ETFs. However, I eventually tired of reading all of the research I deemed necessary to choose and follow individual stocks, and I became frustrated with the headline risk that went with holding individual companies. I found conversing with money managers equally stimulating and, regardless of the good returns our stock portfolio provided, I came to believe that the right combination of managers should give my clients the same or better returns with lower risk because money manager firms could follow many more stocks in more industries and countries than I could. I used mutual funds for the smaller clients and the clients who did not wish to see the individual stocks. I used separately managed accounts for larger clients and those who benefited from seeing the individual holdings of the managers. Segregated funds, also known as guaranteed investment funds (GIFs), are sometimes appropriate for small business owners or professionals who may be vulnerable to lawsuits or potential bankruptcy due to the nature of their business. Eventually, I decided to stop picking and following individual common stocks. I then referred and transitioned the portion of my clientele who wanted to continue to be involved with common stock picking to another advisor where picking stocks continued to be a major part of their service model.

Tax assisted investments: Some advisors look for investments with unique tax features producing large and often immediate tax savings. Over the years there have been many of these investments (resource based and real estate limited partnerships, labour sponsored funds, etc.). Others took advantage of tax loopholes that were later closed. Often the government is allowing such large write-offs to encourage investments in industries with greater than average risk. These investments should be analyzed very carefully and likely recommended only to clients who can afford to lose their after-tax savings investment and who don't require liquidity.

Income trusts: I invested in REITS (Real Estate Investment Trusts) to provide high tax-efficient income and diversification into a different asset class. This diversification was even more important for clients who did not hold any other real estate.

After completing the previous three checklists, the advisor still must select the actual securities, managers, etc. for their product shelf.

Security/Product Shelf
Your final investment security/product shelf will come when you choose specific securities and/or products within the investment delivery vehicles you have selected.

The three previous checklists can be used to create a Client Investment Allocation Decision Flow Chart similar to the one shown earlier to reflect your own choices. Each dotted box on the flow chart refers to a section of the advisor's security/product shelf. The advisor will need to create a short list of individual securities/managers/products for each of those boxes.

Successful advisors usually follow a strict process for identifying the specific securities they will trust with their clients' money. Having completed the previous three checklists, a large part of the process is complete, as you have narrowed your choices to a small group of collections. Finally, you will need to employ screening and analytical processes to choose specific bonds, preferred shares, ETFs, stocks, money managers, real estate, etc. These processes are beyond the scope of this handbook; however, I intend to discuss them in my future handbook about processes and presentations.

You need to have complete confidence that the selections on your security/product shelf suit the purpose intended and that you and your team will be able to follow them well enough to ensure that they continue to serve that purpose.

Investment Platforms
The investment platforms of our industry have evolved considerably over the last 30 years. I believe the move toward fee-based and discretionary platforms is good for many clients and advisors, however not necessarily the best for all clients. The primary importance is the individual client's comfort with whatever platform is employed and that the client knows they are receiving the appropriate amount of value per dollar paid.

The investment platform you employ needs to match the individual client's needs and comfort levels.

Investment Platforms	Service Performer		
	You and Your Team	Outsource	Discretionary
transaction commissions	x		
fee-based	x		x
separately managed accounts (third party)		firm	x
advisor managed accounts (discretionary)	x		x

By the time I retired, we had converted the transaction/commission accounts of most clients to a form of fee-based, including discretionary advisor managed accounts for many clients. Many clients had already grown somewhat comfortable with a fee-based approach through our earlier shift towards managed money for common equities. After we switched to mutual funds and SMAs from individual stock picking, many clients said that it "took the worry out of investing" and that they were happy to be less involved with common stock selection.

I found that the older clients were the most welcoming of advisor managed discretionary accounts, likely for one or both of the following reasons. One: Older clients were likely long-time clients who had plenty of time to develop confidence in us and our approach to investing. Two: Many older clients feared or recognized their current age-related decline in cognitive abilities and wished to rely more heavily on us in the future.

We were happy to keep some or all of an individual client's accounts on the transaction/commission platform to minimize fees and/or keep the client comfortable. I will discuss fee issues in greater detail in the "Pricing and Client Costs Model" and "Advisor Compensation and Career Paths" sections of this book. I will discuss the process of moving clients from transaction-based platforms to managed money, fee-based and discretionary accounts in my future handbook on processes and presentations.

Investment Account Types

Identifying the account types you wish to offer clients is helpful when you are determining the infrastructure you need from your firm or administrative service provider. Some firms will not offer every account type on the list, so you will need to determine if you and your clients can do without the service or find another way to provide it. Some smaller firm's client portfolios will be held at another institution (custodial accounts).

Investment Account Types	Service Performer		
	You and Your Team	Outsource	Discretionary
investment accounts	x	firm	x
investment margin accounts	x	firm	x
third party custodial accounts			
combined investment & banking accounts	x	firm	x
delivery against payment (DAP, DVP)			
receive against payment (RAP, RVP)			
universal life policies	x	external	
Tax-Free Savings Account (TFSA)	x	firm	x
Registered Disability Savings Plan (RDSP)			
Registered Education Savings Plan (RESP)	x	firm	x
Registered Retirement Savings Plan (RRSP)	x	firm	x
Locked-In Retirement Account (LIRA)	x	firm	x
Locked-In Retirement Savings Plan (LRSP)	x	firm	x
Individual Pension Plan (IPP)	x	firm	x
Registered Retirement Income Fund (RRIF)	x	firm	x
Restricted Life Income Fund (RLIF)	x	firm	x
Locked-In Retirement Income Fund (LRIF)	x	firm	x
Life Income Fund (LIF)	x	firm	x
Life annuities	x	external	
donor-advised charitable giving accounts	x	firm	x
multiple currency: _US_EURO_AUS_UK_	x	firm	x

Fortunately, my firm offered every type of account I needed to provide the services I wanted to provide my clients. If necessary, annuities, life insurance and charitable foundations might be outsourceable with your firm's cooperation.

Investment Reporting

All firms will provide the mandatory periodic statements required by the industry. The industry standards must apply to all clients and therefore require too little information for some clients and too much information for other clients. This is very understandable, given the uniqueness of individual clients and the uniqueness of the advisors serving them. Many successful advisors provide additional reports that present the clients' information in a more concise, easier to read format to help clients understand their risk exposures and performance. I expect there are many excellent custom reports that have been created by individual advisors. My downloadable checklist template includes several blank lines for advisors to add their creations.

| Investment Reporting | Service Performer | | |
	You and Your Team	Outsource	Frequency
mandatory statements		firm	4 to 12
online statements		firm	4 to 12
custom portfolio summary	x		1 to 12
performance: minimum required		firm	annually
performance: special reports	x	firm	on demand

Although I was with a large firm that provided many reports in addition to the mandatory statements, I still felt the need to create a custom portfolio summary that provided a more concise portrayal of the client's current investments on one page. We also included reports that showed how we achieved the necessary diversification for that particular client in keeping with our approach to investing and the allocations originally agreed upon with the client. These custom reports were provided during client meetings. Many clients requested that the custom report be sent to them in between meetings (monthly or quarterly). This summary of current investments was often expanded to include investments at other institutions to help us better understand the client's entire situation and to encourage the client to consolidate more of their investments with our group. I intend to explain these reports more thoroughly in my future handbook about processes and presentations.

We also sent numerous firm produced reports to clients relating to performance, monthly income, etc. to suit the individual client's needs and desires.

Tax Reporting for Investments

Year-end tax reporting is an opportunity to add value by helping clients through one of their most stressful tasks. They usually appreciate any help they can get. It is also an opportunity for advisors to add value, strengthen client loyalty and foster a positive relationship with a client's tax accountant. All firms will provide the mandatory year-end tax reporting; however, many successful advisors choose to add some reports that are not automatically sent to clients, such as personalized tax document checklists, realized capital gains reports and summaries of compound interest earned. Throughout the year, advisors may occasionally send reports relating to unrealized gains and year-to-date capital gains. I expect there are other useful reports I have not mentioned here.

| | Service Performer | | |
| | You and | | |
Tax Reporting for Investments	Your Team	Outsource	Frequency
mandatory year-end tax package		firm	annually
personalized client tax document checklist	70%		
custom year-end tax package to client	50%		annually
custom annual tax package to accountant	10%		annually
custom compound bond interest summary	x		annually
YTD capital gain/loss reports	x	firm	as needed
unrealized gain/loss reports	x	firm	as needed

My goal was to minimize the client's effort at tax time and help ensure that the accountants benefited from the tax reporting we provided. My team and I provided additional personalized tax reporting to the clients with more complicated situations that required more paperwork for the government. Of course, these clients were usually our larger clients. Many clients really appreciated our willingness to send all of their tax documents (usually pdfs) to them and/ or their accountants in a customized package. This was especially true of snowbirds. The better your templates and processes for preparing client tax packages, the more the junior members of your team will be able to contribute and the more tax packages you will be able to provide.

If you have recommended investments that cause more paperwork than others, you would be wise to help the client with that paperwork to minimize the client's inconvenience and/ or their accountant's workload. Some accountants will work against you if they find their paperwork onerous because of your choice of investments. This was especially important for the reporting of Separately Managed Accounts. If accountants started preparing tax returns before they had all of our reports, they would do a lot of unnecessary work. Tax preparers usually charge by the hour, so they would sometimes suggest to a client that their tax preparation costs could be greatly reduced by using a different form of investing thereby raising doubts in the client's mind.

Create a Summary of Your Practice's Investment Services

Summarizing the results of your completed investment service model checklists will provide a list of the services you wish to offer to your long-term sustainable clientele and articulate your unique approach to selecting investments. Your summary is also a big step towards providing a "sound intellectual framework for making decisions" as deemed necessary by Warren Buffet in the quote at the beginning of this section.

The following screen shot is the printable listing of all of the items I checked on the sample checklists to identify my practice's investment service model, including space for my comment(s).

The checklist template for creating a similar summary for yourself is included in the business model checklist templates available on my website. The download will also include the sample.

C Timms Sample (Advisor Name)
Summary of Service Model for Investing
Date

Overall Investment Advice Services	You and Your Team	Outsource	Discretionary
determine client's investment goals	x		x
educate: various strategies, securities, etc.	seminar		
educate: expectation of returns & volatility	seminar		
assess client risk tolerance	x		
summarize client financial position/details	x		
make asset class allocation decisions	flow chart		x
provide investment policy statement	x		x
implement (buy/sell investments)	x		x
consider tax effects of recommendations	x	accountant	
year-end tax loss selling	x	accountant	

(Service Performer header spans "You and Your Team", "Outsource", "Discretionary")

Steps: Security Selection for Product Shelf

	You and Your Team	Outsource	Discretionary
select asset class exposure security sets	x		x
select investment strategies	x		x
select investment delivery vehicles	x		x
choose securities for product shelf	x		

Asset Class Exposure Security Sets

Cash & Equivalents Exposure

	You and Your Team	Outsource	Discretionary
high interest savings accounts	x		x
T-bills	x		x
firms' cash management accounts	x		x

Fixed Income Exposure

	You and Your Team	Outsource	Discretionary
GICs	x		x
gov't bonds: federal	x		x
gov't bonds: provincial	x		x
short-term (one to five years)	x		x
compounding bonds/strips	x		x
U.S. bonds	x		x
preferred shares	x		x
insured annuities	x	x	

Common Equities Exposure

common stocks	x	x
all-cap	x	x
large-cap	x	x
Canadian	x	x
U.S.	x	x
international	x	x

Alternatives Exposure

commercial real estate	x	x

Investment Strategies

passive maturity ladder	x	x
equity bottom-up all sectors	x	x
equity bottom-up all countries	x	x
equity style growth	x	x
equity style value	x	x
equity style GARP	x	x
dollar cost averaging	x	
pre-authorized contributions	x	
rebalancing	x	x

Investment Delivery Vehicles

individual high interest savings accounts	x	x
individual t-bills	x	
individual bonds: _fed and prov gov't_	x	x
individual GICs: _CDIC insured_	x	x
individual preferred shares: _big banks_	≥ p2	
initial public offerings: _preferreds_	x	x
mutual funds stocks	x	x
SMA* equity portfolios	x	firm	x
insured annuities personal	x	firm	
insured annuities corporate	x	firm	
income trusts (including REITS)	x	x

Investment Platforms

transaction commissions	x	
fee-based	x	x
separately managed accounts (third party)		firm	x
advisor managed accounts (discretionary)	x	x

Investment Account Types

investment accounts	x	firm	x
investment margin accounts	x	firm	x
combined investment & banking accounts	x	firm	x
universal life policies	x	x	

Investment Account Types (continued)

Tax-Free Savings Account (TFSA)	x	firm	x
Registered Education Savings Plan (RESP)	x	firm	x
Registered Retirement Savings Plan (RRSP)	x	firm	x
Locked-In Retirement Account (LIRA)	x	firm	x
Locked-In Retirement Savings Plan (LRSP)	x	firm	x
Individual Pension Plan (IPP)	x	firm	x
Registered Retirement Income Fund (RRIF)	x	firm	x
Restricted Life Income Fund (RLIF)	x	firm	x
Locked-In Retirement Income Fund (LRIF)	x	firm	x
Life Income Fund (LIF)	x	firm	x
Life annuities	x	x	
donor-advised charitable giving accounts	x	firm	x
multiple currency: _US_EURO_AUS_UK_	x	firm	x

Investment Reporting

			Frequency
mandatory statements		firm	4 to 12
online statements		firm	4 to 12
custom portfolio summary	x		1 to 12
performance: minimum required		firm	annually
performance: special reports	x	firm	on demand

Tax Reporting for Investments

mandatory year-end tax package		firm	annually
personalized client tax document checklist	70%		
custom year-end tax package to client	50%		annually
custom annual tax package to accountant	10%		annually
custom compound bond interest summary	x		annually
YTD capital gain/loss reports	x	firm	as needed
unrealized gain/loss reports	x	firm	as needed

COMMENTS
Approximately 60% of clients have discretionary accounts, expect more as clients age.

Identifying the investment services you wish to offer should help you market your services, train your team and help you determine who on your team will perform the service items.

Review your summary by answering the following questions:

1) Are you trying to do too much?

2) Can you really follow all of the investments?

3) Are you following some investments for only a small number of clients whose revenue does not justify the time spent?

4) Does your firm have all of the infrastructure necessary to offer the investments/services you want to offer? If not, you will need to determine if you can make up for any shortfalls.

Some approaches to investing are more naturally efficient than others. My approach to investing happened to be very efficient from a time management perspective. Diversification gained per hour spent researching and monitoring was much greater when I was picking managers vs picking individual stocks. Choosing only government guaranteed interest-bearing investments required very little ongoing monitoring. Remember that the more investment securities/products on your shelf, the more you must follow to ensure they continue to meet your criteria.

Investment opportunities are constantly changing as the world and the investment industry evolves. An advisor should seek to learn about and take advantage of new investment opportunities while being careful to screen out those that don't fit the criteria of what they wish to offer their compatible clients. The summary of your investment service model will facilitate the screening process. I encourage advisors to customize and add to their checklists as they discover more opportunities and establish more screening criteria.

Determining your approach to allocation decisions and all of the steps you take to select the right investments for your clients involves a lot of work by yourself, your team members and your partners (your firm, money managers, sources of research, etc.). It is important that your clients are given every opportunity to see and recognize this effort, so they understand and value the services they are receiving. Your reporting and communications regarding your efforts and processes relating to investments will add to your credibility and a client's ability to trust you. My experience tells me that more client trust leads to more patience with poor short-term returns and that more patience leads to better long-term results for the clients and all stakeholders of your practice.

Whichever investing strategies and securities the advisor chooses to offer, it will be necessary to develop or adapt efficient methods and processes. It will be important to be consistent yet adaptable and to enjoy the processes involved.

I intend to give advice regarding effective presentations, letters, reports, etc. including examples, templates and methods of communicating your investment approach and services in another handbook for advisors about processes and presentations for clients and prospects. I expect the same book will also describe efficient processes used to select the individual items on your product shelf (stocks, money managers, bonds, preferred shares, GICs, etc.).

Financial Planning Service Model

Financial Planning Should be Part of the Present-Day Financial Advisor's Service Model
I think all financial advisors in the business of serving clients today should consider providing financial planning to their clients. Most clients are happier and more comfortable when they have received some financial planning services, especially those clients approaching or in retirement.

The 2019 Fidelity Retirement Survey published by Fidelity Investments (Canada) asked the survey respondents, "What do you want from your Advisor?" The number one answer on the list (about 83%) was "Helps me to feel comfortable that I will have financial security in the future" (page 11). Most people will need a financial plan to accomplish this feeling of comfort and preparedness.

If you are not currently providing any financial planning services, the thought of incorporating them into your practice may seem overwhelming; however, today's financial planning tools and software make it easier then you may think. Some advisors start with providing retirement projections to satisfy most clients' basic need for financial planning. Many advisors, especially those with smaller teams, use financial planners provided by their firms to create financial plans for their clients. The checklists provided by this book will help these advisors identify the specific financial planning services to be included in their clients' plans.

Financial Planning Services Can Distinguish You from Your Competition

Financial planning is an opportunity for advisors to serve client needs and deepen their relationship with each client, thereby competing favourably with robo-advisors and discount services. The preparation of a financial plan often inspires clients to reveal assets otherwise unknown to the advisor because the client realizes that the accuracy and usefulness of the plan is only as good as the data it is based on, thus providing the advisor with an opportunity to gather more assets. Advisors can add the human element through the gathering of information, interpreting the data and knowing what action to take to help solve issues brought to light during the financial planning process. Financial plans updated annually, or upon significant change in client circumstances, provide visible value to a client. Advisors who don't include financial planning in their business model can expect some, possibly many, of their clients to go elsewhere for their financial plans, and in many cases, their investment business will follow.

History of My Group's Financial Planning Service

Early in my career, I used an Excel spreadsheet to provide my clients with very rough, year by year, forecasts of their liquid assets. This was more than most stockbrokers/advisors provided for many years. As the years went by, I looked at various financial planning software that became available and was disappointed in the presentations they produced for clients. I felt they lacked the detail and clarity necessary to understand the impact of various financial decisions. I also found the graphs too small and lacking the detail necessary to facilitate the decision-making advice I wished to provide. Foolishly, thinking I could not do a great job, I did not offer a proper financial plan for years. I am certain that many clients were feeling the need for a better approach to forecasting even if they did not mention it to me. I began to hear about clients going elsewhere for a financial plan. I think I lost at least two clients and their investment business before I woke up to the fact that an advisor who is looking to take care of their clients' financial needs, should provide thorough and easily understood financial plans to most of their clients.

I started using financial planning (FP) specialists from within my firm to prepare financial plans for my largest clients. I attended and participated fully in all of the meetings between the client and the FP specialist, strengthening the relationship with the clients and learning about financial planning and the process. However, I was uncomfortable with the loss of control and the FP specialist's minimum size criteria. This experience, coupled with the financial planning courses taken by myself and several team members, gave me the confidence to start preparing and presenting the plans without the specialist. I worked for months with a technologically skillful team member and a financial planning software program to create and simplify the presentations for two very different clients who had indicated a strong, immediate desire for improved forecasting. The result was the creation of a detailed template for use with all other clients. A year or so later we created a large graph to provide a simpler presentation of the data.

Bringing the financial planning preparation process into my team gave us the independence to do as many scenarios and updates as we wanted, when we wanted. We were able to prepare more plans for more clients and customize them according to their needs.

Developing and/or Articulating Your Financial Planning Services
In order to develop your practice's financial planning service model, you need to understand the priorities of yourself and your long-term sustainable clientele. What do they want and need, and what will you, the advisor, be comfortable offering? You will already have accomplished this if you created your personal summary of the "Client Service Requirements: Financial Planning" checklist within the "Identify Criteria for Sustainable Individual Relationships" section described earlier in this book.

My sustainable clientele's priorities were retiring comfortably, taking care of their family and sleeping at night. They were looking for financial peace of mind. I showed my clients how they could expect to achieve the financial security they desired for themselves and their family by following the roadmap of their future laid out in our financial plans.

Identifying the financial planning services to offer will help the advisor market their services and determine who will perform and provide the necessary expertise for each service. The checklist will also help an advisor list the features they require in their financial planning software. Note that some advisors use different software for different clients, as simpler, quicker software is sometimes more appropriate for simpler client situations.

The following financial planning service model checklists and related discussions are provided to help advisors identify, describe and analyze the financial planning services they wish to provide to clients:

- Overall Financial Planning Services
- Steps to Provide Financial Planning Services
- Set Realistic Financial Goals
- Year By Year Forecasts
- Budgeting
- Event Expense Planning
- Pre-Retirement Analysis and Advice
- Pension Advice
- Retirement Income and Cash Flow Decisions
- Protection Through Legal Documents
- Protection Through Insurance
- Estate Planning: Preparation Prior to Drafting of Wills
- Estate Planning: Identify Issues to Raise with Lawyer
- Estate Planning: Drafting of Wills
- Special Situations
- Small Business
- Disabled Person Strategies

The checklists include columns to indicate the service performer (advisor and/or team, outsourced within the firm, outsourced externally). As an example, I marked the service items I provided during the last several years of my practice with an "x" or further detail. There is also a column to indicate the frequency of the service. Some of the following sections also include discussions of considerations for completing that section of the checklist and my personal insights into why my approach to financial planning was successful with my clientele. The checklist templates available through my website include spaces to add items that do not appear on the lists.

I recommend including team members in the checklist process as much as their experience and capabilities allow. In the later stages of my career, my team members, especially my associates, were very involved in all aspects of our financial planning service.

Overall Financial Planning Services

The Overall Financial Planning Services checklist will allow you to identify the broad areas of financial planning services that you wish to provide. Each of those areas have a checklist of their own. Many advisors outsource their clients' financial planning to others within their own firm. The more services performed within your group or firm, the less clients will need to go elsewhere for the services they need. You are effectively building a higher fence around your client with each service that you add. There will likely still be a need to refer to other professions (lawyers, accountants, etc.) for special expertise in some areas. Involving yourself by attending meetings or conference calls with your client's experts, where possible, will reinforce your position as their ongoing point of contact for all financial issues.

| | Service Performer | | |
Overall Financial Planning Services	You and Your Team	Outsource	Frequency
set realistic financial goals	x		annually
year by year forecasts	x		annually
budgeting	x		annually
event expense planning	x		annually
retirement planning and advice	x		annually
pension advice	x		annually
retirement income & cash flow decisions	x		annually
protection: legal documents	x		annually
protection: insurance	x		annually
estate planning	x		annually
special situations	x	external	annually
small business	x	external	annually
disabled person strategies		both	annually

Our annual reviews with clients would generally include an updated financial plan and many questions to determine the need for many of the services included on the above list. For example, we would ask about retirement plans, wills, POAs, insurance coverage, etc. Further discussions regarding these agendas will be included in my future handbook on presentations and processes and downloadable templates of these meeting agendas will be available on my website, likely upon completion of the book.

Steps to Provide Financial Planning Services

The more steps in the financial planning process that you and your team provide, the more opportunities you will have to strengthen your relationship with the client. The ability of an advisor to perform the steps varies with the qualifications of themselves and their team as well as the size of their team. The larger your team, the easier it will be to provide more of the steps. As a minimum, I recommend that the advisor and/or their team be involved in the following steps: information gathering, setting and confirming goals and the presentation of the completed plan to the client. An advisor involved in the presentation of the plan and the resulting recommendations will gain and show a greater understanding of the individual client.

| | Service Performer | | |
Steps: Provide Financial Planning Services	You and Your Team	Outsource	Frequency
information gathering	x		annually
setting and confirming goals	x		annually
info input into FP software	x		annually
analysis of forecasts and needs	x		annually
prepare recommendations	x		annually
presentation to client	x		annually
multiple scenarios	x		annually

In my opinion, the advisor or a team member should gather as much of the information as possible. Much of the information is gathered through the normal course of business. We found that we already knew most of the input information required by the financial planning software and only had to ask the client a few questions to augment what we already knew. I was always present when the plan and resulting recommendations were presented to the client, even in my earlier stages of financial planning where the plans were prepared by my firm's financial planning specialist. We would consider updating the financial plan every year for the client's annual review appointment. The continuity gave the clients more confidence and inspired loyalty to our group. Depending on the client's situation, we would usually suggest at least two different scenarios where the resulting forecasts were compared on a detailed graph.

Involvement in the steps also provided my team and I with insights as to how presentations and financial planning services could be improved for the individual and the rest of my clientele.

Including associates will equip them with more understanding and help train them in the purposes, needs and benefits of all of the work that goes into preparing a plan. It will also train them to present plans to smaller clients. Those preparing the plans by inputting and running the program for various scenarios were often less experienced members of our team. It was a wonderful opportunity to learn about the short- and long-term effects of changing circumstances or recommendations. Every client situation was unique. I have provided additional training ideas in the handbook *Team Building for Financial Advisors*.

Our presentations of financial plans were designed to make sure our clients were aware of all the work that went into backing up the numbers and the value they were receiving, even if the clients chose only to review the graph with us. Our efforts were clearly visible. We often mentioned how much it might cost on a per plan basis with a different advisor, whereas financial plans were included in our overall fees.

Set Realistic Financial Goals
Assisting a client in the setting of their financial goals is an excellent opportunity for an advisor to build the relationship with each individual client and to temper unrealistic

expectations. Discussing goals helps to uncover and focus on the client's priorities by compelling the client to think about what they want to spend money on, how much they want to spend in retirement and how much they wish to leave for their heirs. This knowledge should help the advisor and their team relate to the individual client's needs and personalize the advice and service accordingly.

Most of these goals would be established for the client's first financial plan and modified as needed when plans were updated or when the client indicated a change in their circumstances.

Set Realistic Financial Goals	Service Performer		Frequency
	You and Your Team	Outsource	
annual income - working years	x		as needed
lifestyle spending - working years	x		as needed
annual savings - working years	x		as needed
annual income - retirement years	x		as needed
lifestyle spending - retirement years	x		as needed
annual savings - retirement years	x		as needed
debt repayment targets	x		as needed
spending on major events/purchases	x		as needed
return on investments	x		as needed
minimize income taxes payable	x		as needed
minimize estate taxes payable	x		as needed
liquid assets value at specific time	x		as needed
net worth at specific time	x		as needed
estate value for heirs	x		as needed
real estate value	x		as needed

We found that clients would have partially identified their goals and would need our help to fill in the gaps. For example, they might have known how much they wanted to spend in retirement but didn't know how much they needed to save to get there. Or they knew how much they could save each year but didn't know what that would give them in retirement. Many did not know how much they were saving each year and needed our help to figure it out.

Often these goals are revised upon the use of different scenarios in the forecasting process. In many cases actions to achieve one goal will impede another, so running different scenarios through the forecasting software is necessary to understand the full impact of changing situations and/or recommended actions. For example, actions that reduce today's taxes may have a worse than offsetting effect on future years' income taxes or on estate taxes. Conversely, actions taken to reduce estate taxes may be more than offset by a resulting increase on today's taxes. Usually, the client is ultimately looking to maximize total long-term dollars used by themself and/or their family. In any case, our job was to help them make informed decisions.

Year By Year Forecasts
Year by year forecasting provides the simplest answer to most clients' questions regarding future financial security: how much money will I need and have access to during my lifetime, and how much will be left to my heirs when I pass? The year by year forecasting of financial planning programs available will provide this in varying degrees of detail and accuracy. Different programs provide different levels of input and output. An advisor's challenge is to determine how much detail/depth does each client need their forecasting to provide and then find the program that will do as much as possible for them, as efficiently as possible.

The following checklist is intended to show potential year by year forecasted items that the advisor may wish to provide their clients in their financial plan presentations and/or include in the backup for the totals provided in their presentations. Once again, there is room on the template to provide additional items.

Year By Year Forecasts	Service Performer		
	You and Your Team	Outsource	Frequency
forecast by individual	x		as needed
forecast by household	x		as needed
forecasts include companies	x		as needed
lifestyle spending	x		always
annual savings non-registered	x		as needed
annual savings TFSA	x		as needed
annual savings RRSP	x		as needed
annual savings RESP	x		as needed
sources of external cash flow	x		always
government income (CPP, OAS)	x		always
sources of self-financed cash flow	x		always
income taxes payable	x		as needed
OAS clawback	x		as needed
liquid assets value (total)	x		always
liquid assets value by acct type	x		always
investment asset class allocations	x		always
expected return (changing risk tolerance)	x		always
life insurance cash surrender value	x		as needed
outstanding debts	x		as needed
real estate value	x		as needed
net worth	x		always
costs of final arrangements (funeral, etc.)			
estate taxes (cap gains, RRSP/RRIF, etc.)	x		as needed
probate fees	x		always
estate after-tax value	x		as needed
graphs	x		as needed

In the later years of my practice, we offered detailed financial plans to all clients that incorporated almost all of the items listed above. I am certain that the preparation of these financial plans led to higher client satisfaction and retention. Long standing clients told me, "We look forward to seeing the updated financial plans". I think they were referring primarily to the year by year forecasts, especially after we developed the accompanying graphs illustrating multiple scenarios. I expect to include more detail regarding our financial planning services in my future handbook about processes and presentations.

Budgeting

Budgeting	Service Performer You and Your Team	Outsource	Frequency
provide budget template			
estimate annual spending	x		as needed
plan for saving	x		as needed
plan for tax installments	x		as needed
plan for charitable giving	x		as needed
provide expense analysis			
provide debt analysis	x		as needed
provide mortgage review	x		as needed
provide budget review			

We did very little line by line expense budgeting with clients; although, we did send links or provide printouts of budget templates for their use. We were most likely to work backwards with their income and saving numbers to estimate how much they were spending in a year.

Event Expense Planning

Event Expense Planning	Service Performer You and Your Team	Outsource	Frequency
home purchase or sale	x		as needed
vacation property purchase/sale	x		as needed
large item purchase (car, etc.)	x		as needed
education	x		as needed
religious event	x		as needed
special trip	x		as needed
wedding	x		as needed
divorce			

We were always sure to ask about potential life events and large item purchases that would affect client's finances so we could include them in year by year forecasting and make recommendations on how to best save for and make the funds available when needed. Once again, an advisor will have to choose a financial planning program that allows for the year by year input of expected event expenses they wish to include in their client's plans.

Retirement Planning and Advice

The same Fidelity retirement survey mentioned earlier indicated that 88% of pre-retirees with a written financial plan felt prepared for retirement compared to only 43% of those without a plan (page 10 of survey).

I have created checklists covering the advice and services clients may need regarding pre-retirement and pensions as well as retirement income and cash flow decisions to help them feel prepared for their future retirement years. I expect there are current and future issues I have not listed and expect advisors to add their own items to the checklists accordingly.

Pre-Retirement Analysis and Advice

| | Service Performer | | |
| | You and | | |
Pre-Retirement Analysis and Advice	Your Team	Outsource	Frequency
retirement goals	x		annually
retirement financial needs	x		annually
retirement income	x		annually
savings strategies (how much, when)	x		annually
savings allocation decisions (account type)	x		ongoing
use of registered accts (TFSAs, RRSPs, etc.)	x		ongoing
designate beneficiary/successor annuitant	x		as needed
potential loss of employer benefits			
evaluation early retirement package	x		as needed

Clients often seek the magic number of how much they need to support their lifestyle in retirement. What-if scenarios in the year by year forecasts should be able to provide a reasonable range of expectations.

Pension Advice

Pension Advice	Service Performer		Frequency
	You and Your Team	Outsource	
group pension plans (investments, etc.)	x		as needed
pension plan choices (investments, etc.)	x		as needed
IPPs (independent pension plans)	x		rare
compare: pension, locked-in RRSP, annuity	x		as needed
risk analysis of corp. pension (funding, etc.)	x		rare
risk analysis of senior exec retirement plan	x		rare
spousal survivor pension benefits	x		as needed

Clients were often faced with decisions regarding their company pension plans. Some clients would ask for help choosing investment options in their defined contribution pension plan. Others asked us about defined benefit versus defined contribution plans and how much they should contribute themselves. We were often asked to help them choose between pension payout options upon retirement. Once again, what-if scenarios in year by year forecasting helped provide the analysis needed to answer many of the pension advice questions.

We were happy to help clients, where possible, to ensure their pension decisions aligned with their overall investment and retirement planning goals. Since different plans have different features, we could not know what would be asked next, but we wanted our clients to come to us to help them sort out whatever choices they had, so we could help them decide within the context of their overall financial and personal situation. This also helped us maintain our position as their primary source of financial advice.

Retirement Income and Cash Flow Decisions

Retirement Income & Cash Flow Decisions	Service Performer		
	You and Your Team	Outsource	Frequency
OAS timing decision	x		as needed
CPP timing decision	x		as needed
CPP income splitting	x		as needed
company pension benefit start date	x		as needed
company pension income splitting	x		as needed
timing of RRSP conversion to RRIF	x		as needed
RRIF/LIF, etc. withdrawal decisions	x		as needed
RRIF/LIF, etc. vs annuity decisions	x		as needed
unlocking LIF/LRIF pension plans	x		as needed
deregistering RRSP/RRIF	x		as needed

We would sometimes run a few forecasts to compare the long-term effects of different retirement income and cash flow decisions.

Protection Through Legal Documents

Legal Documents	Service Performer		
	You and Your Team	Outsource	Frequency
provide names of lawyers to draft POA(s)	x		on request
consider suitable POA attorney(s)	x		as needed
consider institutional POA attorney	x		as needed
assist preparation prior to drafting POAs	x		as needed
draft POA personal care		external	as needed
draft POA financial		external	as needed
review POA(s) personal care			
review POA(s) financial			
prenup or cohab agreement			
postnup agreement			
trusts for married adult children			

We would always ask the clients if they had any of the above documents. We would ask for the date of POA documents and discuss their choice of attorney(s) encouraging them to consider the current age, situation and expected capabilities of the appointed attorneys and estate trustees/executors. We welcomed and encouraged opportunities to meet the attorneys and trustees. Where appropriate, we suggested the use of institutions to fill these vital roles. Near the end of my career, I offered to accompany clients to sessions with their lawyers for wills and POAs. I found that clients were particularly grateful for this service. I also recommend that advisors have a list of trusted estate lawyers to refer clients to.

Clients may not realize that a POA attorney has the ability to move their investment accounts to another advisor with whom the client does not have a relationship. To avoid this, a client can request that the lawyer drafting the POA include a clause requiring that a particular investment advisor(s) be retained.

Reminding a client of the importance, and assisting a client in the preparation, of drafting POAs will protect the client and possibly the advisor's relationship with the client. Approximately 15 years before I retired, a client of mine for 10 years suffered a severe stroke. A neighbor of hers, whom I had never heard of, walked into the hospital and convinced my client to sign a POA. The newly appointed POA attorney immediately transferred my client's accounts to a discount broker and refused to talk to myself and the client's good friend who had been helping her with her finances for all of the 10 years that I knew her. As far as we knew, the client had never established a POA prior to her stroke and had no blood relatives that we were aware of. No one appeared to have legal standing to question the POA. Needless to say, after that experience, I became more insistent that my clients have POAs.

Protection Through Insurance

Insurance	Service Performer		
	You and Your Team	Outsource	Frequency
life insurance needs analysis	x	firm	as needed
term life	x	firm	as needed
whole life (permanent)	x	firm	as needed
disability	x	firm	as needed
critical illness	x	firm	as needed
long-term care			
extended health care			
property: home or tenant			
auto			

We helped clients determine how much term life insurance they needed to protect their family from a loss of income caused by an unexpected death, by using year by year forecasting to show the financial effects of one spouse's death. We ran a financial plan with input data based on the surviving spouse's expected income and assets after the death of their spouse. We showed how much the survivor would have to live off of and prepared multiple scenarios showing the effects of adding life insurance proceeds to the survivor's non-registered assets. These were very effective "what-if" scenarios.

Estate Planning

I believe that both the client and the advisor will benefit from the involvement of the financial advisor in the client's estate planning process. An advisor's help identifying issues and preparing for the client's meeting with a lawyer regarding the drafting of their will should provide the client with more confidence and peace of mind. The process will deepen an advisor's understanding of their client and their long-term goals. The involvement will reinforce the client's view of the advisor as their ongoing point of contact for all financial issues and may open the door to meeting or learning more about the next generation and the client's other trusted advisors (lawyers, accountants, etc.). Advisors who don't involve themselves in a client's estate planning are more vulnerable to losing the client and their investment business to another advisor who does or an advisor with a good relationship with the client's lawyer or accountant.

In the last few years of my practice, I offered to spend time with some clients discussing their estate planning. Many clients will appreciate this assistance. This is especially important for elderly clients with few or no trusted and capable relatives or who simply do not want to involve close family members. After I had sat with an elderly widow and her lawyer through the whole will making process, including introducing her to a trust company to act as her executor/trustee, she told me, "It is a huge weight off my shoulders to finally have this done. I am relieved!". I expect that I would have continued to assist many more clients with their estate planning needs if I had continued to practice.

I recommend attempting to build a relationship with the client's estate lawyer. If they don't have an existing relationship, you should provide them with a short list of lawyers you have a relationship with to choose from. This will help to build a fence around the clients and might ensure continuation of the relationship when their POA is activated or if a trust for their heirs is involved. This will give clients additional peace of mind and help you grow and protect your business.

Preparation Prior to Drafting of Wills
Many lawyers will provide "intake forms" requesting personal and financial information and lists of materials for clients to bring to the first meeting to discuss their will. The completion of such forms, in addition to the information provided in many financial plans, will shorten the time spent on gathering information and allow the client and their lawyer to focus their time on issues and strategies. Advisors should review the lawyer's intake form and consider adding details unique to the

client, for example, listing of digital assets or RESPs for which the client is a subscriber.

Preparation Prior to Drafting of Wills	Service Performer You and Your Team	Outsource	Frequency
assess need to update will	annually		
review existing will		x	
provide names of lawyers to draft will(s)	as needed		
list of all financial assets/obligations	as needed		
list of insurance policies with details	as needed		
provide questionnaire of personal info.	as needed		
prepare list of personal assets (art, etc.)			
prepare list of digital assets			

Our up-to-date financial plans and appointment agendas contained much of the financial information a lawyer needs to efficiently prepare a will that meets a client's objectives. If I was practicing today, I would find or prepare a checklist of potential digital assets including social media, health records, personal photos, e-mail, notes, etc. The checklist could be used by the client to instruct their executor regarding the treatment of the assets (distribute, delete or deactivate).

Identify Issues to Raise with Lawyer

Advisors who understand many of the potential issues faced by a client's estate and heirs will be well equipped to help their clients identify relevant issues to bring to their lawyer's attention. The checklist below identifies many of these issues. It also provides topics an advisor could seek to learn more about through courses, books and industry periodicals.

Identify Issues to Raise with Lawyer	Service Performer		Frequency
	You and Your Team	Outsource	
consider suitable executors/trustees	x		
consider institutional executor/trustee	as needed		
consider executor/trustee fees	x		
probate taxes	x		
Cdn. taxes at death (cap gains, RRSPs, etc.)	x		
U.S. taxes at death (real estate, securities)	x		
international taxes at death (real estate)			
life insurance (whole or universal life)	x	firm	
vacation property transition strategies	x		
legal obligations (alimony, child support)			
heirs capability of handling inheritance	x		
potential need for testamentary trusts	x		
maximize wealth transfer	x	firm	
small business transition			
Corporate Estate Bond	x	firm	
charitable giving	x		
digital assets			
subscriber rights for RESPs	x		
maintain investment advisor relationship	x		

Throughout the financial planning process, we would often identify potential issues for a client to raise their awareness and give them a chance to think about their feelings before they were in front of their estate lawyer making decisions regarding the content of their will. Our detailed financial plans also provided estimates of death taxes, estate values, etc.

Identifying issues for the clients to raise with lawyers is a valuable service clients will appreciate that will likely set you apart from the competition. We saw a situation where the failure to designate an RESP successor subscriber resulted in a significant delay in the funding of a student's education while the same student was dealing with the death of his parent. If I was practicing today, I would be sure to remind clients that many lawyers will suggest a clause in a will to determine how their digital assets are to be managed after the client's death.

Many of our clients had difficulties choosing executors/trustees for their wills. They were unable to think of people they trusted who were willing, in good health or the right age. In these situations, we recommended an institution. Many clients assumed that trust company executor fees were very expensive; however, we were relieved to learn that trust company fees were actually less than we had seen some private individuals charge. I remember an individual executor who charged the highest fee allowed by law for an extremely simple estate involving only the selling of the investment portfolio and minor personal assets. It is possible that the client intended the executor's fee as a gift in itself; however, the fee was not predetermined in the will, so the executor was free to charge up to the maximum. In any case a client should not dismiss institutional executors based on assumptions relating to fees, and I think it is wise for the fees to be clarified by the will.

Some of our clients with wills creating testamentary trusts inserted a clause to name us as the investment advisor of choice. Note that many estate trustees, especially trust companies, will automatically transfer the investment accounts if an investment advisor is not named in the will.

Drafting of Wills

| | Service Performer | | |
| | You and | | |
Drafting of Wills	Your Team	Outsource	Frequency
attend will preparation meetings	on request		on request
draft primary will		external	
draft secondary will(s) (business, intl, etc.)		external	
review will(s)	on request	x	

In the later years of my career, I volunteered to accompany clients to their will planning sessions with their lawyers. The clients really appreciated having the "second brain in the room". I found my relationship with the client deepened significantly. I also strengthened relationships with lawyers I already knew and gained new relationships with others. Attending these sessions taught me more about estate planning and potential issues. This knowledge helped me identify potential issues and determine what services I should provide to help other clients in the future.

Special Situations

Clients occasionally find themselves in new stressful and/or demanding situations where they need and appreciate support from a trusted advisor. This is an opportunity for the financial advisor to take the lead, perhaps going above and beyond the norm to serve the client's immediate needs and to reduce the client's stress. This will deepen their relationship with each client when they are feeling vulnerable, and help the advisor compete favourably with robo-advisors and discount services.

Special Situations	Service Performer		
	You and Your Team	Outsource	Frequency
severance issues	x		as needed
divorce			
death in family	x		as needed
severe illness in family	x		as needed
client named as POA	x		as needed
client named as executor	x		as needed

We would listen to the client describe their new and stressful situation and often discovered ways we could help them, before the client even knew what to ask us for. We would give lists (provided to us by partners) of their potential duties to new POA attorneys and estate executor/trustees. We would also make suggestions regarding the need for specialized advice from their other professionals (lawyers, tax accountants, etc.). Many clients mentioned to us years later how much they appreciated our help in their time of need.

Small Business

Small Business	Service Performer		
	You and Your Team	Outsource	Frequency
key person insurance			
protect from marriage breakdown			
succession (unexpected event)			
succession for retirement			
income smoothing	x	external	as needed
corporate estate bond	x	external	as needed

Our experience with small business was primarily with holding companies and professional corporations. We employed Corporate Estate Bonds as a tax-efficient strategy to wind down a corporation through the use of life insurance.

Disabled Person Strategies

Working effectively for households with disabled persons often requires specialized knowledge and experience uncommon for most financial advisors. Some firms are more equipped than others to provide the services these clients might need.

Disabled Person Strategies	Service Performer		
	You and Your Team	Outsource	Frequency
Registered Disability Savings Plan			
lifetime benefit trusts			
qualifying trust annuities			
qualified disability trusts			
Henson trusts			
gov't disability support programs			
income tax credits			
RESP ramifications			

Create a Summary of Your Practice's Financial Planning Services

Summarizing the results of your completed financial planning service model checklists will provide a list of the services you wish to offer to your long-term sustainable clientele and articulate your unique approach to financial planning.

The following screen shot is the printable listing of all of the items I checked on the sample checklists to identify my practice's financial planning service model, including space for my comment(s). The checklist template for creating a similar summary for yourself is included in the business model checklist template available on my website. The download will also include the sample.

C Timms Sample (Advisor Name)
Summary of Financial Planning Service Model
Date

Overall Financial Planning Services	Service Performer You and Your Team	Outsource	Frequency
set realistic financial goals	x		annually
year by year forecasts	x		annually
budgeting	x		annually
event expense planning	x		annually
retirement planning and advice	x		annually
pension advice	x		annually
retirement income & cash flow decision	x		annually
protection: legal documents	x		annually
protection: insurance	x		annually
estate planning	x		annually
special situations	x	external	annually
small business	x	external	annually
disabled person strategies		both	annually

Steps: Provide Financial Planning Services			
information gathering	x		annually
setting and confirming goals	x		annually
info input into FP software	x		annually
analysis of forecasts and needs	x		annually

Steps: Provide Financial Planning Services (continued)

prepare recommendations	x		annually
presentation to client	x		annually
multiple scenarios	x		annually

Set Realistic Financial Goals

annual income - working years	x		as needed
lifestyle spending - working years	x		as needed
annual savings - working years	x		as needed
annual income - retirement years	x		as needed
lifestyle spending - retirement years	x		as needed
annual savings - retirement years	x		as needed
debt repayment targets	x		as needed
spending on major events/purchases	x		as needed
return on investments	x		as needed
minimize income taxes payable	x		as needed
minimize estate taxes payable	x		as needed
liquid assets value at specific time	x		as needed
net worth at specific time	x		as needed
estate value for heirs	x		as needed
real estate value	x		as needed

Year By Year Forecasts

forecast by individual	x		as needed
forecast by household	x		as needed
forecasts include companies	x		as needed
lifestyle spending	x		always
annual savings non-registered	x		as needed
annual savings TFSA	x		as needed
annual savings RRSP	x		as needed
annual savings RESP	x		as needed
sources of external cash flow	x		always
government income (CPP, OAS)	x		always
sources of self-financed cash flow	x		always
income taxes payable	x		as needed
OAS clawback	x		as needed
liquid assets value (total)	x		always
liquid assets value by acct type	x		always
investment asset class allocations	x		always
expected return (changing risk tolerance)	x		always
life insurance cash surrender value	x		as needed
outstanding debts	x		as needed
real estate value	x		as needed
net worth	x		always
estate taxes (cap gains, RRSP/RRIF, etc.)	x		as needed
probate fees	x		always

Year By Year Forecasts (continued)

estate after-tax value	x		as needed
graphs	x		as needed

Budgeting

estimate annual spending	x		as needed
plan for saving	x		as needed
plan for tax installments	x		as needed
plan for charitable giving	x		as needed
provide debt analysis	x		as needed
provide mortgage review	x		as needed

Event Expense Planning

home purchase or sale	x		as needed
vacation property purchase/sale	x		as needed
large item purchase (car, etc.)	x		as needed
education	x		as needed
religious event	x		as needed
special trip	x		as needed
wedding	x		as needed

Retirement Planning

Pre-Retirement Analysis and Advice

retirement goals	x		annually
retirement financial needs	x		annually
retirement income	x		annually
savings strategies (how much, when)	x		annually
savings allocation decisions (account type)	x		ongoing
use of registered accts (TFSAs, RRSPs, etc.)	x		ongoing
designate beneficiary/successor annuitant	x		as needed
evaluation early retirement package	x		as needed

Pension Advice

group pension plans (investments, etc.)	x		as needed
pension plan choices (investments, etc.)	x		as needed
IPPs (independent pension plans)	x		rare
compare: pension, locked-in RRSP, annuity	x		as needed
risk analysis of corp. pension (funding, etc.)	x		rare
risk analysis of senior exec retirement plan	x		rare
spousal survivor pension benefits	x		as needed

Retirement Income and Cash Flow Decisions

OAS timing decision	x		as needed
CPP timing decision	x		as needed

Retirement Income and Cash Flow Decisions (continued)

CPP income splitting	x		as needed
company pension benefit start date	x		as needed
company pension income splitting	x		as needed
timing of RRSP conversion to RRIF	x		as needed
RRIF/LIF, etc. withdrawal decisions	x		as needed
RRIF/LIF, etc. vs annuity decisions	x		as needed
unlocking LIF/LRIF pension plans	x		as needed
deregistering RRSP/RRIF	x		as needed

Protection

Legal Documents

provide names of lawyers to draft POA(s)	x		on request
consider suitable POA attorney(s)	x		as needed
consider institutional POA attorney	x		as needed
assist preparation prior to drafting POAs	x		as needed
draft POA personal care		external	as needed
draft POA financial		external	as needed

Insurance

life insurance needs analysis	x	firm	as needed
term life	x	firm	as needed
whole life (permanent)	x	firm	as needed
disability	x	firm	as needed
critical illness	x	firm	as needed

Estate Planning

Preparation Prior to Drafting of Wills

assess need to update will	annually		
review existing will		on request	
provide names of lawyers to draft will(s)	as needed		
list of all financial assets/obligations	as needed		
list of insurance policies with details	as needed		
provide questionnaire of personal info.	as needed		

Identify Issues to Raise with Lawyer

consider suitable executors/trustees	x		
consider institutional executor/trustee	as needed		
consider executor/trustee fees	x		
probate taxes	x		
Cdn. taxes at death (cap gains, RRSPs, etc.)	x		
U.S. taxes at death (real estate, securities)	x		
life insurance (whole or universal life)	x	firm	

Identify Issues to Raise with Lawyer (continued)

vacation property transition strategies	x		
heirs capability of handling inheritance	x		
potential need for testamentary trusts	x		
maximize wealth transfer	x	firm	
Corporate Estate Bond	x	firm	
charitable giving	x		
subscriber rights for RESPs	x		
maintain investment advisor relationship	x		

Drafting of Wills

attend will preparation meetings	on request		on request
draft primary will		external	
draft secondary will(s) (business, intl, etc.)		external	
review will(s)	on request	x	

Special Situations

severance issues	x		as needed
death in family	x		as needed
severe illness in family	x		as needed
client named as POA	x		as needed
client named as executor	x		as needed

Small Business

income smoothing	x	external	as needed
corporate estate bond	x	external	as needed

COMMENTS

We have completed financial plans for every client that was interested.
We usually updated the financial plan as part of the client's annual review.

Identifying the financial planning services you wish to offer should help you choose your financial planning software, market your services, train your team and help you determine who will perform the service items.

Review your summary by answering the following questions:

1) Are you trying to do too much?

2) Are you and/or your team qualified to perform all of the services you have marked?

3) Will your financial planning services help your clients answer the question "Will I have financial security in the future?"

4) Should you offer the services to all of your clients or only those whose revenue justifies the time spent?

5) Does your firm offer assistance in financial plan preparation or other resources related to financial planning?

I encourage advisors to customize and add to their checklists. Periodically reviewing the checklists and your summary is important, as more opportunities and needs relating to financial planning are likely to arise as clients' needs evolve, tax rules change and advances in technology enable advisors to do more.

The financial plan document can be overwhelming to clients. Although it is very important that clients see the work that has been done, it is more important that they can quickly understand their situation and the actions they need to take. We found the use of a large graph showing explanations of inflection points to be most helpful.

Whichever financial planning services the advisor chooses to offer, it will be necessary to develop or adapt efficient methods and processes. It will be important to be consistent yet adaptable and to enjoy the processes involved. Remember, if you don't offer financial planning services, you may be in danger of losing your client to another advisor who will.

This series' future handbook on processes and presentations will give advice regarding effective presentations, graphs, letters, reports, etc., including examples, templates and methods of communicating your financial planning approach and services.

Tax Return and Tax Strategies Service Model

An advisor needs to decide how much attention to pay to clients' tax issues. The degree to which an advisor addresses their clients' taxes will vary from advisor to advisor depending on the qualifications of the advisor and others in their team or firm.

Tax Return Services

| | Service Performer | | |
| | You and | | |
Tax Return Services	Your Team	Outsource	Frequency
see Tax Reporting for Investing checklist	x		
prepare year-end tax returns			
answer accountant's questions	x		as needed
access to trusted tax experts		x	as needed
referral list: trusted tax accountants	x		as needed

I had no interest in preparing tax returns but would gather extra information to help the client's tax expert at tax time. Some advisors' firms include formal tax advice and tax return preparation as part of their service. I expect their clients find this to be very convenient. However, I have seen instances where the separation of responsibilities has resulted in the exposure of either negligent or inappropriate advice by the investment advisor or the accountant. As a result, I believe that clients are better protected by having separate professionals who can consult with each other but are not otherwise aligned with each other's practices, thereby eliminating potential conflicts of interest.

We would recommend that clients hire professionals to do their taxes. An advisor should have a ready-made list of trusted quality tax accountants to refer upon request. The list should include accountants of various hourly rates, personalities and specialties (small business, professional, estate planning, etc.).

Tax Strategies

The checklist below identifies some commonly used tax strategies that advisors might employ with some or all of their clients. It also provides topics an advisor could seek to learn more about through articles, courses, books, etc.

Tax Strategies	Service Performer		Frequency
	You and Your Team	Outsource	
consult accountants: proposed action effect	x	x	as needed
timing of gains and losses	x	external	as needed
tax loss selling	x	external	annually
income splitting strategies	x	external	
timing and allocation of reg. acct. contrib	x	external	
spousal loan for income splitting	x	external	as needed
income and expense timing	x	external	
charitable giving: in-kind donations	x	external	as needed
donor advised charitable foundations	x	external	as needed
holding companies special considerations		external	
trusts special considerations		external	
family trusts		external	
estate freezes		external	
farm properties		external	

Regardless of my accounting background, I recognized that "I did not know what I did not know" and that full-time tax accountants would be more up to date on current tax issues and the client's overall tax situation. We were happy to build relationships with our clients' accountants based on a win-win-win scenario. I was grateful to have the client's tax expert available to bounce ideas off, especially when we were investing for a client's corporate account.

I was always sure to understand the tax impact of my recommended changes to clients' portfolios, as well as the ongoing tax impact of the securities I recommended. My team and I educated ourselves on tax issues by reading periodicals and articles from our firm or partners (mutual funds and insurance companies). We looked for potential tax saving strategies, like those listed above, as we worked with the client throughout the year. We would then contact the accountant to discuss the strategy's potential application to a particular client's situation. Many clients only spoke to their accountants at tax time, when the accountants were extremely busy, unless we suggested an inquiry mid-year.

Create a Summary of Your Practice's Tax Services

Summarizing the results of your completed tax service model checklists will provide a list of the services you wish to offer to your long-term sustainable clientele and articulate your unique approach to tax services.

The following screen shot is the printable listing of all of the items I checked on the sample checklists to identify my practice's tax service model, including space for my comment(s). The checklist template for creating a similar summary for yourself is included in the business model checklist template available on my website. The download will also include the sample.

C Timms Sample (Advisor Name)
Summary of Service Model for Tax Services
Date

Tax Return Services	You and Your Team	Outsource	Frequency
see Tax Reporting for Investing checklist	x		
answer accountant's questions	x		as needed
access to trusted tax experts		x	as needed
referral list: trusted tax accountants	x		as needed

Tax Strategies	You and Your Team	Outsource	Frequency
consult accountants: proposed action effect	x	x	as needed
timing of gains and losses	x	external	as needed
tax loss selling	x	external	annually
income splitting strategies	x	external	
timing and allocation of reg. acct. contrib	x	external	
spousal loan for income splitting	x	external	as needed
income and expense timing	x	external	

Service Performer spans the "You and Your Team", "Outsource", and "Frequency" columns.

Tax Strategies (continued)

charitable giving: in-kind donations	x	external	as needed
donor advised charitable foundations	x	external	as needed
holding companies special considerations		external	
trusts special considerations		external	
family trusts		external	
estate freezes		external	
farm properties		external	

COMMENTS (continued)

I have no interest in preparing tax returns.

I do all I can to work with, assist and provide info to client's tax professionals.

I am always looking for tax strategies that may be appropriate for our clients.

Review Your Complete Service Component

An advisor's completed summaries of their communication, investing, financial planning and tax services should fully articulate the advisor's unique service model. While reviewing their service model in its entirety, an advisor should answer the following questions:

1) Are you confident that your unique service model goes well beyond what clients would receive from robo-advisors or discount investment service providers?

2) Does your service model help you achieve your overall mission and fulfill your commitment to clients?

3) Does your service model contain many or all of the attributes of a successful service model listed below (explained in greater detail earlier in this book)?

   – services match compatible, sustainable clientele requirements

   – narrows the advisor's focus

   – visibility of advisor and team effort and expertise

   – services must be reliable, timely and accurate before offered to all clients

   – affordable for clients and advisor

- scalable to many clients
- repeatable to the same client
- advisor enjoys their time at work
- background work for services easily delegated or outsourced
- advisor is proud of their service
- fosters strong relationships with clients
- flexible and evolving

Teams and firms will benefit from understanding an advisor's unique business model. Team members will learn what services they will be expected to provide, helping them become proficient and knowledgeable in providing those services. An advisor's firm management will be able to easily see how the advisor plans to operate their practice and the type and risk level of investments they will be using.

Service Model is Always a "Work in Progress"
An advisor's unique service model should always be considered a "work in progress". What may have been a unique service in the past, often becomes the new standard of expected service for your clients and the industry. To keep and please loyal clients, an advisor's level of service must continue to expand and the efficiency for providing services must improve to keep costs down. Your new and expanded services must be demonstrated and/or communicated to clients to prove that the value they are receiving justifies their costs. Be aware that clients of many years may take what their advisor does for granted, not realizing that many advisors do not provide the same services. Your client presentations should go a long way to proving your value. Your processes will help you provide services efficiently and effectively.

An advisor should keep an eye on what the competition is doing and respond accordingly. Sometimes this means adding a service, other times it means explaining why you should not do what the competition is doing, and sometimes it means clarifying why what you are doing accomplishes the same goals in better ways.

Listen closely to your compatible, sustainable clients. They often tell you what your service model should include, especially if you read between the lines of their comments and questions. When a client requests a service outside your current business model, you should ask yourself if enough of your clients would benefit from the same service to justify the resources required to develop and provide that particular service.

An advisor should consider reviewing their service model at least once per year.

Completing these checklists may have inspired you to offer more services for your clients. You may be wondering how to accomplish this efficiently and effectively. My handbook on team building and my future handbook on practice processes and presentations give advice and many examples to help you provide the services you wish to offer.

Component 3: Processes for Streamlining Delivery of Services and Practice Management

The use of systematic processes and templates by yourself and your team will enable efficient delegation and supervision of the performance of many of the activities needed to find and service your sustainable client base and help you run your practice. During my career, my team and I developed many detailed processes for all six of the business model components with an emphasis on the major categories of the service model (communication, investing, financial planning and tax). These processes along with a good contact management system allowed me to grow my clientele and expand both my team and services. I intend to discuss processes for streamlining each business model component in great detail in my future presentations and processes handbook. My website provides downloadable templates and samples for the processes and presentations discussed in all of the handbooks.

Component 4: Determine Needed Resources and Suppliers/Sources

Similar to any small business, an advisor, especially a revenue sharing advisor, must identify the resources they need to perform the processes required to deliver their unique service model to their clientele. Next, an advisor needs to determine what resources they have ready access to through their firm and external sources. The advisor must then determine how much of their personal resources they are willing to spend on their practice and how to best spend it to fill in the gaps.

Every advisor's most important resource is their own time. All other resources need to be managed to maximize the use of the advisor's time. The advisor's firm is likely the greatest source of these resources. The advisor should explore what resources the firm provides and seek ways to use them or modify them to fit their unique service model efficiently and effectively. Advisors in large firms can explore other departments for potential tools and deeper expertise relating to their service model. External sources include product providers, such as money managers, software providers and industry associations. All advisors will have access to tools and/or templates provided by their professional associations (e.g. Canadian Institute of Financial Planners) and independent advisor coaches. Identifying and wisely using these resources should allow the advisor to provide more services and serve more households while minimizing how much of their own money is required.

The advisor's most controllable resource is the use of their own money. There were many occasions during my career when I saw the need for software, hardware, marketing, practice management tools, more team members, etc. Sometimes the need was unique to my practice, and sometimes my firm was not willing to spend the money, so I had to spend my own money on my practice. I realized that waiting for the firm to invest in my practice would limit my ability to grow and/or serve my clients. In many cases I spent my money to effectively buy time for myself and/or my team. Most successful advisors I know have spent a significant amount of their own money on their practice.

Identify Needed Resources and Potential Sources

I have created a checklist to help advisors identify the resources needed and available to them through their firm or external sources. Some of the services provided by the firm will cost the advisor additional funds. Costing of the resources is outside the scope of this book, although I expect an advisor could modify the checklist to help them quantify potential costs. Once again, I have used the last year of my practice as an example.

The checklist groups resources/expenses into the following categories:

- Software Programs and Tech Tools
- Team
- Training and Education of Advisor and Team
- Client Education
- Marketing
- Investment Research
- Specialists
- Office

In my practice, I felt that the use of technology and my team were my most important resources in the provision of client services. Software and templates enabled my team and myself to offer more services to more people very effectively and efficiently. They increased productivity thereby increasing capacity. Software programs and tech tools were also integral to maximizing the use of resources in other checklist groupings.

Software Programs and Tech Tools

Software Programs and Tech Tools	Need	Source		
		Available from Firm	Advisor Paid Created or Modified	External Supplier
contact management	x	x	x	Goldmine
tax reporting	x	x	x	
portfolio reporting	x	x	x	
performance reporting	x	x		
financial planning program (in depth)	x	FP Solution	x	
financial planning program (quick)		Razor		
every day templates, macros, etc.	x	x	x	
monthly/quarterly statements	x	x		
practice evaluation reports	x	x	x	

Contact management system:

Does the firm's contact management system satisfy client, team and advisor needs? A good contact management system is crucial for efficient delegation and effective client service. It must have a unique record for each client that shows, by date and time, all past and future notes, activities and e-mails with the advisor and all team members. It should also provide a daily list of tasks for each team member, including both client specific and non-client specific actions. The system should also include calendars for each team member linked to client records when relevant. I chose a contact management system that allowed me to customize fields and reports to reflect my unique clientele and practice needs. I expect to discuss contact management systems more thoroughly in a future handbook about processes and presentations.

Financial planning software:

Advisor financial planning software needs to relate directly to the individual advisor's financial planning service model. Some advisors use different programs for different clients, based on how complicated the individual client's situation is and the level of detail needed. I felt the need to add my customized graphs to enhance the output given by the program provided by my firm. I expect to discuss this graph and my financial planning processes more thoroughly in a future handbook about processes and presentations.

Search for existing processes/templates:
An advisor who is constantly looking for more efficient and more effective ways to deliver services will be able to serve more clients effectively and profitably. Low-cost or free templates/ checklists, etc. are likely available through their firm, external product suppliers, such as mutual fund companies or advisor coaches such as myself. I always found the modifiable processes and templates to be the most useful.

Create your own processes, templates and macros:
Many advisors, especially those with skilled teams, will take the time to create their own processes, macros and templates when they see an unfulfilled need. Whenever I noticed that a team member or I was repeating a task many times, we considered developing a template or a macro to both save time and minimize mistakes.

Team
An advisor needs to continually assess the number of team members and the team member capabilities needed to fulfill the advisor's ambitions relating to client service and practice growth. A firm's human resources department and branch administrator can be very helpful in the recruiting and hiring process when you help them understand what you are looking for.

		Source		
Team	Need	Available from Firm	Advisor Paid Created or Modified	External Supplier
team member salaries	x	3	3.5	
team member bonuses	x	0	6.5	
team appreciation events	x	x	x	
gifts to team members	x		x	

Team size, hiring, training, structure, compensation, team member duties and team management are explored thoroughly in my *Team Building for Financial Advisors* handbook. My website provides templates and samples of team member duty lists including overviews of team time spent in the various services, etc. that will help the advisor determine if the time spent correlates with the intended focus of the practice.

Training and Education of Advisor and Team

Training/Education:Advisor & Team	Need	Source		
		Available from Firm	Advisor Paid Created or Modified	External Supplier
software	X	X	X	X
marketing	X	X	X	X
practice management	X	X	X	X
client communication	X	X	X	X
investing	X	X	X	X
financial planning	X	X	X	X
tax	X	X	X	X

Most advisors have many sources of training and education including their firm and external providers, such as industry associations, periodicals and money management firms—all provide seminars and articles. Money management firms and periodicals were also an excellent source of insight into financial industry trends and practice management techniques. I was and still am a subscriber to the *Investment Executive* and major Canadian newspapers and often read the *Advisor's Edge* magazine.

Client Education

Large firms and money managers create many useful information pieces for distribution by advisors to their clients. Sometimes these information pieces are sent to all advisors, however many are not. An advisor should explore their firm's intranet and external supplier websites or speak to contacts within their firm and external suppliers to find the educational material applicable to their clients.

Client Education	Need	Source		
		Available from Firm	Advisor Paid Created or Modified	External Supplier
mutual fund reports	x	x	x	x
separately managed acct reports	x	x	x	x
common stock reports		x		x
market history reports	x	x	x	x
RRSP, RRIF, TFSA, RESP info	x	x		x
life insurance strategy info	x	x	x	x
income replacement info	x	x		x
estate planning strategy info	x	x		x
POA, executor, trustee info	x	x		x
tax strategy reports	x	x		x
government budget reports	x	x		x

My firm and external money managers provided many client education pieces. Insurance companies provided us with information pieces regarding strategies relating to life insurance, disability and annuities. I often included stock market history or economic analysis research provided by my firm or a money manager in my client communications to help clients be patient during bear markets.

Marketing
Website and newsletter builders and brochures vary from firm to firm. Some firms are very flexible, allowing advisors to choose from various formats and create much of their own content. Others require advisors to conform to strict format and content requirements.

Marketing	Need	Source		
		Available from Firm	Advisor Paid Created or Modified	External Supplier
website builder	x	x	x	
newsletter builder		x		
newsletter content		x	x	mny mgrs
brochures online	x	x	x	
brochures printed		partial	x	
client appreciation events	rare	partial	very rare	
client gifts	x		x	
Andex Charts	x			fund cos

Fortunately, my firm allowed me the flexibility of format and content while providing a workable structure to personalize my website.

Investment Research

Investment Research	Need	Source		
		Available from Firm	Advisor Paid Created or Modified	External Supplier
mutual fund analysis	x	x		x
money manager due diligence	x	x	x	x
common stocks (in-house)	rare	x		
preferred shares (in-house)	x	x		
corporate bonds (in-house)		x		
in-house screening program: _____				
client online access to research	x	x		
client online screening of research				
Bloomberg	x	x		
external screening program: _CPMS_				
external source: _ Credit Suisse_	rare	x		
external source: _ Value Line_	rare	x		

When I was picking stocks and/or money managers, I used research from my firm and other sources my firm provided. I would look for ways to compare the relevant data effectively eliminating or ranking many potential picks through screening processes. I expect to discuss stock picking and money manager selection processes in greater detail in a future handbook about processes and presentations.

Specialists

Every practice will rely on various specialists based on the level of expertise and experience of the advisor and their team members as well as the service model of the practice.

Specialists	Need	Source		
		Available from Firm	Advisor Paid Created or Modified	External Supplier
insurance	X	X		
financial planner		X		
trust and estate planning	X	X		X
legal	X	X		X
tax	X	X		X

I was licenced to provide advice on insurance but still relied on insurance specialists within the firm for assistance and experience. I would occasionally call upon our firm's specialists for financial planning, trust and estate planning assistance with issues where I lacked experience. We would generally discuss legal or tax issues with the lawyers or accountants of the particular client in question.

Office

Your office space and equipment should encourage teamwork, efficiency and productivity as well as project professionalism. Your office environment should be a healthy, pleasant place for your clients to visit and for you and your team to work. Providing advisors and team members with the ability to work from home through remote access is more and more important as technology improves the quality and speed of access. Remote access provides advisors and team members with flexibility to work at home especially when personal situations might otherwise prevent or reduce productivity. Remote access also provides a valuable backup plan for uncontrollable world and local events, such as pandemics, natural disasters and terrorist activity.

Office	Need	Source		
		Available from Firm	Advisor Paid Created or Modified	External Supplier
real estate: _location, space_	x	x		
advisor private office	x			
home office	x		x	
remote access: _advisor & team_	x	x	x	
computer hardware	x	x		
furnishings	x	x	x	
printers, fax, scanners, etc.	x	partial	partial	
office materials	x	partial	partial	
mail services	x	x		
courier services	x		x	

When I finally earned the right to a private office, I enjoyed the privacy for phone calls with clients and privacy for meetings with clients or team members. I also enjoyed the peace and quiet when I needed time to think. I am absolutely certain that having a private office increased my productivity, my peace of mind and my credibility with my clients. Remote access motivated me to work more if I was at home when I had a great idea I wanted to act on immediately, when I wanted to check my email or when I had some idle time I wished to use more productively. Remote access also allowed me to take time away from the office, knowing I could access everything I needed immediately if necessary. Team members with children could work from home when a child was ill. I know many advisors who would work from home or their cottage occasionally to avoid commute time.

Create a Summary of Your Needed Resources and Potential Sources

Summarizing the results of your completed resource allocation decision checklists will provide a list of the resources you need and who will supply them.

The following screen shot is the printable listing of all of the items I checked on the sample checklists to identify my "needed resources and potential sources model" including space for my comments. The checklist template for creating a similar summary for yourself is included in the business model checklist template available on my website. The download will also include the sample shown in this book.

C Timms Sample (Advisor Name)
Summary of Needed Resources and Potential Sources
Date

		Source		
Software Programs and Tech Tools	**Need**	**Available from Firm**	**Advisor Paid Created or Modified**	**External Supplier**
contact management	x	x	x	Goldmine
tax reporting	x	x	x	
portfolio reporting	x	x	x	
performance reporting	x	x		
financial planning program (in depth)	x	FP Solution	x	
every day templates, macros, etc.	x	x	x	
monthly/quarterly statements	x	x		
practice evaluation reports	x	x	x	

Team

team member salaries	x	3	3.5	
team member bonuses	x	0	6.5	
team appreciation events	x	x	x	
gifts to team members	x		x	

Training/Education: Advisor & Team

software	x	x	x	x
marketing	x	x	x	x
practice management	x	x	x	x
client communication	x	x	x	x
investing	x	x	x	x
financial planning	x	x	x	x
tax	x	x	x	x

Client Education

mutual fund reports	x	x	x	x
separately managed acct reports	x	x	x	x
market history reports	x	x	x	x

Client Education (continued)

RRSP, RRIF, TFSA, RESP info	x	x		x
life insurance strategy info	x	x	x	x
income replacement info	x	x		x
estate planning strategy info	x	x		x
POA, executor, trustee info	x	x		x
tax strategy reports	x	x		x
government budget reports	x	x		x

Marketing

website builder	x	x	x	
brochures online	x	x	x	
client appreciation events	rare	partial	very rare	
client gifts	x		x	
Andex Charts	x			fund cos

Investment Research

mutual fund analysis	x	x		x
money manager due diligence	x	x	x	x
common stocks (in-house)	rare	x		
preferred shares (in-house)	x	x		
client online access to research	x	x		
Bloomberg	x	x		
external source: _ Credit Suisse_	rare	x		
external source: _ Value Line_	rare	x		

Specialists

insurance	x	x		
trust and estate planning	x	x		x
legal	x	x		x
tax	x	x		x

Office

real estate: _location, space_	x	x		
advisor private office	x			
home office	x		x	
remote access: _advisor & team_	x	x	x	
computer hardware	x	x		
furnishings	x	x	x	
printers, fax, scanners, etc.	x	partial	partial	
office materials	x	partial	partial	
mail services	x	x		
courier services	x		x	

COMMENTS
I was sure to recognize events in client's lives (death in family, etc.) with a gift or donation.

Although compliance officers are not identified in any of the above checklists, they are a valuable resource to all advisors. Adhering to compliance policies and learning from and working with compliance officers may feel time consuming; but in the long run, the avoidance of client complaints and legal problems is well worth it.

I tried to take full advantage of the resources supplied by my firm. I would often supplement or modify whatever the firm provided without having to "reinvent the wheel". Over the years I found that my firm provided more and more of the resources that I required to provide my clients with the services I felt they needed. I also took advantage of tools and services offered by external sources, such as money manager firms and industry associations. The best tools allowed me to download data to Excel or Word allowing me to customize and modify presentations or formats to suit my clientele and my practice.

In my experience, the most successful advisors spend their own money on their business, often "buying time" for themselves and their team, while also taking full advantage of services provided by their firm and external sources.

Component 5: Pricing and Client Costs Model

A good pricing/client cost model will benefit all concerned. Clients and advisors should both believe that the pricing and costs are fair, thereby resulting in a sustainable, win-win relationship. In a successful pricing model, clients believe that they are receiving good value for their dollar, and the advisor feels they are being fairly compensated for their effort and expertise. A good pricing model will naturally align the interests of the advisor with their client such that the advisor benefits or suffers alongside their client and that the advisor's success is contingent on the success of their client. The advisor is also responsible for minimizing clients' total costs and ensuring that clients receive good value for all costs incurred. Whichever model the advisor chooses they should understand the effectiveness of their approach in relation to the following attributes.

Attributes of Pricing and Client Cost Models
1) Alignment of client and advisor interests

    a. Correlation to success of recommendations

    b. Correlation to advisor and advisor's team effort

2) Ease of explanation to clients
3) Transparency and visibility of fees and costs to the client
4) Consistency from period to period

The pricing and client cost model should identify all the costs the client will incur relating to the services offered by the advisor including direct and indirect charges. Direct charges are paid directly by the client to the advisor's firm and are visible on statements or transaction confirmations. Indirect charges include revenue received by the advisor's firm relating to client accounts as well as investment expenses that are deducted from investments but not visible on client statements or transaction confirmations. Full transparency of all a client's fees and costs, and a clear understanding of how an advisor is paid, is crucial to the maintenance of a long sustainable relationship between the advisor and the client.

The financial advice industry's fee/commission structures have evolved into a variety of approaches with variable pricing within those approaches. Fee structures for each firm, and advisors within each firm, can be very different. For example, the same mutual fund can often be purchased with many different fee structures (back-end, front-end, low-load, F-series, etc.). Many advisors will employ a variety of combinations of fee structures/ pricing models to fit their individual clients and the investment products and services they offer.

Develop and Articulate Your Approach to Pricing and Client Costs

In order to develop your practice's approach to pricing and client costs, you need to understand what your long-term sustainable clients want and need to be comfortable. They should feel they are receiving good value for their dollar. You will already have accomplished some of this if you completed the "Client's Comfort and Preferences Regarding Payment for Advice and Service" checklist described earlier in this book (Step 2 of Component 1 *Identify the Most Compatible Clients for your Practice*).

I have created the following flexible checklists (template available for downloading on my website) for potential approaches to pricing and client costs models to help advisors articulate, modify or design their pricing model. An advisor using the downloaded template will need to fill in explanations, amounts and percentages to articulate their unique fee structure. They can modify lines to help them fully describe what their clients pay to the advisor's firm and service providers. As an example, I have identified the pricing and client costs I employed the last year of my practice. The following sections will also give my views relating to the effectiveness of each approach in relation to the potential attributes mentioned.

Direct Charges
I have identified the following forms of potential direct charges and created separate checklists for each.

- Transaction/Trading Charges
- Advisor Annual Fee % Based on Client Assets
- Fee Only (hourly, annual or fee-for-service)
- Fee-based on Performance
- Administration/Operating Charges

Transaction/Trading Charges
Under a transaction and trading approach to charging clients, the client pays a commission upon completion of a transaction. Generally, these charges occur with purchases of investments but don't always occur with sales. (Maturities and redemptions are often commission free, especially for fixed income securities.) Commissions generally correlate with the size of the trade. The use of transaction and trading charges has been declining steadily as more advisors switch to a fee-based approach. Advisors who were surveyed for both the 2019 *Investment Executive* (*IE*) Brokerage Report Card (BRC) and Dealers' Report Card (DRC) indicated, on average, that transaction-based revenue accounted for less than 25% of the overall gross revenue that they earned in the previous 12 months. For the surveys, "brokerage" advisors are those who work for firms that are exclusively IIROC-registered (major bank-owned brokerages as well as national and regional independents) while "dealer" advisors are those who work for

firms that are either dual-registered (IIROC and MFDA) or exclusively MFDA-registered — referred to in the Report Card (RC) as either full-service or mutual dealers.

The effectiveness of a transaction and trading approach is discussed below in relation to the potential attributes of pricing and client cost models.

1) Alignment of client and advisor interests:

   a. Correlation to success of recommendations:

   When the amount of the commission is aligned with the value of the trade, the advisor's and client's interests are somewhat aligned as successful recommendations lead to higher client assets, which lead to higher value trades, which lead to higher commissions for the advisor. Successful recommendations will often result in new deposits from existing clients as well as referrals leading to more future transaction commissions. However, an advisor who trades infrequently will be paid less than an advisor who trades frequently regardless of how the portfolio performs for the client.

   b. Correlation to advisor and advisor's team effort:

   An advisor is paid for the effort of determining that a change should be made and for implementing the change. However, an advisor is not paid for their time, research, thought and expertise required to determine that a client should continue to hold existing investments. A commissioned advisor is not paid for their time, research, thought and expertise involved in deciding against potential investments. Also, a commissioned advisor is not paid on some transactions, for example, the redemption of a bond or mutual fund, although they will likely be paid when the proceeds are reinvested.

2) Ease of explanation to clients:

The triggering of transaction costs is usually simple to explain as the client relates the advisor's efforts to explain and complete the transactions to the immediate cost of the transaction. The calculation of transactions can be as simple as the advisor wishes. The original regulated stock commissions calculations were based on the price of the stock and the quantity of shares purchased or sold. Today, for simplicity, many advisors charge a percentage of the total trade value or a flat dollar rate per trade.

3) Transparency and visibility of fees and costs to the client:

Industry regulators are requiring more visibility of transaction costs. Generally, the visibility of transactions and trading charges is very high, although firms will vary regarding the visibility of these costs on trade confirmations and monthly statements as well as year-end summaries.

4) Consistency from period to period:

Clients' year to year transaction costs are dependent on the investment strategies employed by the advisor. Some fixed income strategies, like a bond ladder, will be very consistent whereas the amount of trading in an equity portfolio can vary dramatically from year to year even though the advisor is working just as hard on client service, research, etc.

There are many successful advisors using a transaction-based pricing and client cost model with strong, sustainable client relationships where both the client and the advisor are happy with the approach.

Direct Charges

Commission/Transaction/Trading Charges	Incurred	Frequency
purchase of bond _0.2%/yr, max 1%_	x	at execution
sale of bond _0 - 0.2%/yr, max 1%_	x	at execution
purchase of preferred share _0.2%/yr, max 1%_	x	at execution
sale of preferred share _0.2%/yr, max 1%_	x	at execution
buy common stock _min $140 , max 1% (unsol)_	occasional	at execution
sale common stock _min $140, max 1% (unsol)_	occasional	at execution
options _____		
futures _____		
mutual fund front end _____		
commission: _____		
commission: _____		
commission: _____		
mutual fund switch or change fees: _____		
mutual fund redemption fees	rare	at execution

I began my career in 1983 when the price and client cost model was primarily transactional for most advisors. Bonds were quoted at a price including the transaction cost that was determined by the advisor and was not visible to clients. Mutual fund clients were charged up front non-negotiable commissions on purchases. Stock commissions were regulated and based on the price of the stock and the quantity of shares purchased or sold. As stock commissions became negotiable, discount brokers emerged and soon threatened to take the clients who felt capable of picking their own investments.

I think many advisors who are still transactional are so because they and their clients are familiar with and accustomed to the transaction-based approach. Client accounts that involve very little trading and little other service may be best suited to the transaction-based approach. However, as non-transaction services have grown, transaction costs may not be enough to fairly compensate advisors for their work which may include financial planning, regular reviews, personalized reporting, etc.

As I approached the end of my career, most of my clients were fee-based, but some clients also had a non-fee-based account to hold stocks they wished to own (outside my recommended portfolios).

A real danger for a transaction-based advisor is the potential perception of a salesperson relationship instead of a professional advisor relationship. The very word "commission" has its origin in sales. If an advisor is receiving a commission, they are in danger of being perceived as a salesperson who benefits from the volume of trades and who may be tempted to trade for the sake of commissions instead of client's best interests.

Advisor Annual Fee % Based on Client Assets

Under the fee based on asset value approach to charging clients, the client pays a regular, periodic fee (usually monthly or quarterly) calculated as a percentage of the value of their portfolio at that time. Fee rates, methods of calculation and frequency of charges will differ among firms and advisors. Some will charge the same percentage rate on all of the assets, and others will charge different rates for assets in different asset classes. Most will have graduated rates based on the asset size of the account/household. Often fee-based accounts will have a minimum charge affecting smaller accounts, thereby increasing the percentage cost to smaller accounts and sometimes causing clients to leave the advisor for a more affordable approach. The 2019 *IE* Advisors' RC indicated that advisors surveyed for both the Brokers' RC and Dealers' RC said, on average, that fee and/or asset-based revenue accounted for more than 70% of the revenue they earned in the previous 12 months.

The effectiveness of a "fee-based on assets approach" is discussed below in relation to the potential attributes of pricing and client cost models.

1) Alignment of client and advisor interests:

   a. Correlation to success of recommendations:

      When the client's fees are based on the value of the client's assets, both the client and the advisor benefit from increases in the value of the client's accounts. Conversely, both the client and the advisor suffer from decreases in the value of the client's accounts. As a result, the advisor's interests are naturally aligned with the client, and the client is likely to see their advisor as "on their side of the table".

   b. Correlation to advisor and advisor's team effort:

      An advisor will be paid for their time, research, thought and expertise regardless of the number of trades recommended in the investment portfolio. They will also be paid for services unrelated to investing, such as financial planning, personalized reporting, etc. The advisor will need to communicate with their clients in ways that ensure the client can readily see evidence of the advisor's effort. An advisor charging different rates for different asset classes is likely doing so because their approach to a particular asset class requires less effort.

2) Ease of explanation to clients:

Regular, periodic fees based on asset values are fairly simple to explain to clients. The calculation of client costs is very simple when the fee is one rate charged on the total of all assets managed. When different rates are charged for different asset classes, the calculation becomes more complicated. The advisor should keep in mind that the more categories with different rates, the more complicated the calculation becomes, and the harder it will be for clients to understand.

3) Transparency and visibility of fees and costs to the client:

Fees based on asset values are usually very transparent as they are shown on regular account statements as they are charged.

4) Consistency from period to period:

Fees based on asset values will rise and fall with the assets but are generally more consistent than transaction/trading costs.

The advisor will have to decide when and how often the client will be charged. Monthly charges are smaller and less of a shock to clients, especially for the initial fee period. Monthly charges will provide the advisor with consistent monthly pay; however, cash may have to be raised every month for the fee. Quarterly charges will also provide consistent pay, but the advisor will receive their pay once every three months.

Advisor Annual Fee % Based on Client Assets	Incurred	Frequency
% based on total of all assets managed: _____		
cash: _0.0%_	x	quarterly
gov't guaranteed bonds/GICs: _0.2%_	x	quarterly
preferred shares: _0.2% big bank rate reset_	x	quarterly
common stock picking: _____		
equity mutual funds: _1.0% F-series_	x	quarterly
balanced mutual funds: _____		
fixed income mutual funds: _____		
separately managed equity: _1.5% - 2.25%_	x	quarterly
separately managed fixed income: _____		
minimum annual: _$2,000 ($0 advisor managed)_	x	quarterly

I believe that an advisor's approach to charging clients has a strong influence on the client's perception of the advisor as a professional versus a salesperson. I always strove to be perceived as a professional on par with accountants and lawyers. As a result, I welcomed methods of charging clients that were not based on transactions or commissions. I preferred the fee-based approach over fee-for-service or an hourly rate, because I wanted to be free to do whatever I thought the client needed (e.g. multiple financial plans), without having to convince the client that the cost was worth it.

A "fee-based on assets" advisor will need to ensure that clients see value for the fees they pay. We accomplished this through the services already described in the other components of the business model. We also made an effort to help clients reduce their accounting fees through tax reporting and their legal fees by providing financial planning information to their estate lawyers.

I believe that most fee-based advisors employ the "percent based on total of all assets managed" approach, and I can see the advantage in the simplicity of doing so. It also removes any perception of bias towards particular asset classes. However, I chose to charge clients less for fixed income because my government guaranteed maturity ladder strategy was very passive and required less effort. I had always charged 0.2% per year commission for the purchases of bonds in the five-year bond ladder and did not want clients to be paying more under my fee-based approach to pricing and client costs. This approach to fixed income also resulted in a lower overall fee for most households, making us more competitive.

In hindsight I probably undercharged for preferred shares. When I decided on the pricing, I thought the big bank rate reset preferred shares would perform similar to the government bonds and GICs and that the preferreds would be held until the redemption date without the need for much monitoring or decision making. I was very wrong as they proved to be much more volatile and required much more ongoing thought, research and monitoring than originally expected.

The continuous research, monitoring and communication with clients regarding their equity investments justified a higher client fee (vs fixed income). I priced our fees for mutual funds at the same rate as the trailers we were previously receiving from the back-end and front-end versions of the same funds. The separately managed account fee was all-inclusive with very flexible pricing that I was able to customize to each client based on size, etc. The client's total costs for a separately managed account was usually less than the total costs for a mutual fund.

When I converted my clients to fee-based, I initially charged my clients monthly. However, after a few years, I realized that I could reduce related admin work (checking fees, raising cash for fees) by two thirds and reduce the number of admin calls to my clients by changing from monthly to quarterly fees. Clients were also less likely to be affected by minimum fees with quarterly charges. I expect to discuss converting transaction-based clients to fee-based in greater depth in my future handbook on processes and presentations.

The danger for a "fees based on assets" approach, especially for clients who are used to the transactional approach, is a client's fear that the advisor will be less likely to contact them since the advisor will not be rewarded with an immediate payout upon making a call.

If the advisor is fee-based, the team compensation incentives will be clearly aligned with clients, if the team's compensation has a high component of sharing in the practice's revenue. My *Team Building for Financial Advisors* handbook discusses team compensation in depth.

Fee Only (hourly, annual or fee-for-service)
Under a "fee only" approach to charging clients, the client pays an hourly fee, an annual flat fee, a fee for a particular service (e.g. a financial plan), or a combination of the three. Some advisors who use "transactional and trading charges" or the "fee-based on asset value" approaches may charge stand-alone

fees for financial plans. Those charging a flat annual fee might bill monthly or quarterly. The 2019 *IE* Brokerage RC indicated that advisors surveyed for that report said fee-for-service revenue accounted for 2.2% of the revenue that they earned in the previous 12 months. Advisors surveyed for the 2019 *IE* Dealers' RC said fee-for-service revenue accounted for 1.8% of the revenue that they earned.

The effectiveness of a fee only approach is discussed below in relation to the potential attributes of pricing and client cost models.

1) Alignment of client and advisor interests:

   a. Correlation to success of recommendations:

   There is very little correlation between the fees charged to the client and the effects of the advisor's recommendations on their portfolios or financial well-being, although a happy client may use their services again or send them more referrals.

   b. Correlation to advisor and advisor's team effort:

   There is a very direct correlation between the fee and the advisor and advisor's team effort as the advisor is paid by the job as it is completed.

2) Ease of explanation to clients:

   Fees are very easily explained and calculated.

3) Transparency and visibility of fees and costs to the client:

   Fees are clearly documented, likely with an invoice and/or shown on regular statements.

4) Consistency from period to period:
   The client will determine how often and how many services they require. Their fees will vary accordingly.

Fee Only (hourly, annual or fee-for-service)	Incurred	Frequency
hourly rate: $_(range)_		
flat charge for year: $_____		
preparation of initial financial plan: $_(range)_		
update of financial plan: $_(range)_		

The hourly and/or fee-for-service approach compares well with the professional billings of lawyers and accountants. However, I believe this approach may hamper the free and fluid communication needed to sustain a continuous long-term relationship.

Although I strove to be thought of as a professional equal to lawyers and accountants, I also wanted to control the quality of my service without needing the client's approval for the hours needed to do so. Under the fee-for-service approach, if a client is reluctant to pay a separate fee for a financial plan, our ability to fully understand and give advice would be restricted. We liked preparing multiple scenarios and regular updates without charging our clients extra. We would often run a plan to quantify the benefits of a proposed investment or life insurance strategy. We also welcomed client calls with questions or fears about their investments or financial situation, and they welcomed our calls, knowing that the calls were not going to trigger additional costs for them. I expect they would be hesitant to call if they knew the hourly fee clock would start ticking the moment we picked up the phone.

The annual flat fee would allow the advisor to control their services and would allow the free and fluid communication needed to sustain a continuous long-term relationship. The advisor would need to consider raising the fee as their costs increased with inflation, etc.

The danger of a fee only (hourly or fee-for-service) approach is that a client may not receive the best and most comprehensive financial advice because they may be choosing the service offered based on the hours required or the cost of the particular service item.

Fee Based on Performance

Generally, "fee based on performance" calculations are percentages of the positive returns of the client's investment portfolio. These fees may be in addition to a base flat fee or asset-based fee. I believe some advisors will reduce future year's fees to compensate for losses of previous years. I believe some performance fees are based on the performance in relation to an agreed upon benchmark(s). I have not known any advisors who use a performance-based approach to charging for their services, although they might recommend money managers/mutual funds whose funds charge performance fees that should be identified in their pricing and client costs model.

The effectiveness of a fee based on performance approach is discussed below in relation to the potential attributes of pricing and client cost models.

1) Alignment of client and advisor interests:

   a. Correlation to success of recommendations:

   The fee is usually highly correlated with the success of recommendations.

   b. Correlation to advisor and advisor's team effort:

   An advisor/money manager is paid much less, and possibly nothing, when the portfolio suffers losses even if those losses are due to severe stock market conditions. The fees do not reflect how hard the advisor is working to maintain a high level of service.

2) Ease of explanation to clients:

   The ease of explanation will depend on how complicated the method of calculation is and could range from extremely simple to very complex.

3) Transparency and visibility of fees and costs to the client:

I have no experience with these fees, and I can't even be sure if the fees are direct or indirect.

4) Consistency from period to period:

The fee has the potential to vary dramatically from year to year.

Fee Based on Performance	Incurred	Frequency
% based on return: _(description)_		

I was never comfortable with the fee based on performance approach for my fees nor for any managed money or investment products.

There are numerous dangers to this approach. An advisor who is depending on performance fees, may go out of business during tough years where they receive very little pay, leaving a client with no advice when the client will need it the most. Advisors and managers are often incented to take more risk as the advisor/manager usually participates much more in profits than losses. Many funds with performance based fees with "catch up" clauses have closed after bad years and reopened under a different name, so they don't have to reduce their future fees because of past losses, thereby fully participating in the clients gains and avoiding participation in the losses.

Administration/Operating Charges

Administration and operating charges have been created by firms to cover administrative needs including those for special accounts. In recent years firms have also created small household fees and inactivity fees to recover the bookkeeping costs of issuing statements for accounts that don't generate much revenue, probably hoping to discourage advisors from maintaining relationships with unprofitable clients.

An advisor usually has very little control over these charges; however, they must be included in the pricing and client costs model as they are part of the client's total costs. The advisor should look for ways to minimize the administration/operating charges where possible.

Administration/Operating Charges in relation to the potential attributes of pricing and client cost models are discussed below.

1) Alignment of client and advisor interests:

   a. Correlation to success of recommendations: There is very little correlation.

   b. Correlation to advisor and advisor's team effort: There is very little correlation.

2) Ease of explanation to clients:

   These costs are usually very straight forward and explained in standard account documents.

3) Transparency and visibility of fees and costs to the client:

   These fees are usually shown clearly on client statements.

4) Consistency from period to period:
   These fees are usually very consistent from year to year.

Administration/Operating Charges	Incurred	Frequency
admin fee (RRSP, RRIF, LIF, etc.): _$125_	x	annually
TFSA fee: _$75 ($0:fee-based/assets >$100,000)_	rare	annually
RESP fee: _$75 ($0:fee-based/assets >$100,000)_	rare	annually
small household fee: _($125-$250)_	rare	annually
inactivity fee: _____		
special account fee: _$200 ($0 if fee-based)_	rare	annually
transfer out fee: _$100_	x	annually
banking fee (wiring, etc.)	x	on execution
safekeeping fees (paper certificates): _____	rare	annually
interest charged on margin accounts: _____		
custodial fees		
admin fee: _____		

Indirect Charges

Indirect charges include revenue received by the advisor's firm relating to client accounts as well as investment expenses that are deducted from investments but not visible on client statements or transaction confirmations.

Indirect Charges	Incurred	Frequency
trailing commissions (mutual funds, ETFs)	x	monthly
fees embedded in financial products (GICs, etc.)	x	on execution
fees embedded in currency conversion		
back-end fund purchase commission: _____		
product fees (commission paid by supplier)	rare	on execution
fund management fees	x	
mutual fund MERs: _1.0% - 1.35%_	x	
mutual fund trading fees (TER)	x	
new issue commissions paid by issuer	x	on execution
fees embedded in life annuity products	x	on execution
fees embedded in life insurance products	x	on execution
referral fees: _advisor pays for receiving referral_	rare	varies
finders fees: _ advisor paid for finding a mortgage_	rare	on execution

I tried to avoid indirect charges because of the lack of transparency of the fees. I did not want a client to feel misled about their full costs relating to any of my recommendations. I took advantage of opportunities to make fees more visible to clients. Where statements did not show the fees, we tried to show them in our own customized fee disclosure reports. The template and explanations relating to this report will likely be found in my future handbook on processes and presentations.

Create a Summary of Your Practice's Pricing and Client Costs Model

Summarizing the results of your completed pricing and client costs model checklists should help you articulate your approach to charging clients for services and include all of your clients' direct and indirect costs for the services you provide.

The following screen shot is the printable listing of all the items I checked on the sample checklists to identify my practice's pricing and client costs model during my final year, including space for my comment(s). The checklist template for creating a similar summary for yourself is included in the business model checklist template available on my website. The download will also include the sample.

C Timms Sample (Advisor Name)
Summary of Pricing & Client Costs
Date

Direct Charges

Commission/Transaction/Trading Charges	Incurred	Frequency
purchase of bond _0.2%/yr, max 1%_	x	at execution
sale of bond _0 - 0.2%/yr, max 1%_	x	at execution
purchase of preferred share _0.2%/yr, max 1%_	x	at execution
sale of preferred share _0.2%/yr, max 1%_	x	at execution
buy common stock _min $140 , max 1% (unsol)_	occasional	at execution
sale common stock _min $140, max 1% (unsol)_	occasional	at execution
mutual fund redemption fees	rare	at execution

Advisor Annual Fee % Based on Client Assets		
cash: _0.0%_	x	quarterly
gov't guaranteed bonds/GICs: _0.2%_	x	quarterly
preferred shares: _0.2% big bank rate reset_	x	quarterly
equity mutual funds: _1.0% F-series_	x	quarterly
separately managed equity: _1.5% - 2.25%_	x	quarterly
minimum annual: _$2,000 ($0 advisor managed)_	x	quarterly

Administration/Operating Charges		
admin fee (RRSP, RRIF, LIF, etc.): _$125_	x	annually
TFSA fee: _$75 ($0:fee-based/assets >$100,000)_	rare	annually
RESP fee: _$75 ($0:fee-based/assets >$100,000)_	rare	annually
small household fee: _($125-$250)_	rare	annually
special account fee: _$200 ($0 if fee-based)_	rare	annually
transfer out fee: _$100_	x	annually
banking fee (wiring, etc.)	x	on execution
safekeeping fees (paper certificates): _____	rare	annually

Indirect Charges	Incurred	Frequency
trailing commissions (mutual funds, ETFs)	x	monthly
fees embedded in financial products (GICs, etc.)	x	on execution
product fees (commission paid by supplier)	rare	on execution
fund management fees	x	
mutual fund MERs: _1.0% - 1.35%_	x	
mutual fund trading fees (TER)	x	
new issue commissions paid by issuer	x	on execution
fees embedded in life annuity products	x	on execution
fees embedded in life insurance products	x	on execution
referral fees:_advisor pays for receiving referral_	rare	varies
finders fees:_ advisor paid for finding a mortgage_	rare	on execution

COMMENTS

I gradually changed most clients to fee-based (over 70%).

Some clients have kept a transaction account for their own stock picking.

The review of the checklists may prompt an advisor to change or modify their existing approach to pricing. Are the clients being charged fairly based on the effort expended by the advisor and their team? Before modifying an existing pricing model, an advisor will need to consider how big the change will be for each individual client. The advisor should be able to understand how the fee structure might impact the client-advisor relationship as well as quantifying the potential annual dollar change. Change can be very difficult when the client and/or advisor is comfortable with the existing approach.

"Appendix B: Why Many Full-Service Independent Revenue Sharing Advisors Have and Deserve Above Average Incomes" will remind revenue sharing advisors of the value they bring to their clients through the long-term advisor-client relationship. Many of the discussions put forth in Appendix B may help some advisors justify their fees to clients.

———

Full transparency of all a client's fees and costs and a clear understanding of how an advisor is paid is crucial to the maintenance of a long sustainable relationship between an advisor and their client. Upon completion of these checklists, an advisor will have identified their approaches to charging the client and all of the client's costs. This is an important initial step to providing the needed fee and cost transparency. Whatever fee approach you use, you need to be able to explain it to your clients with clarity and conviction. I intend to discuss fee explanations and presentations in more detail in my future handbook on processes and presentations.

Component 6: Advisor Compensation and Career Paths

I have written this section to help all advisors, including experienced advisors whose compensation structure is established and those new to, or wishing to join, the business. I hope to help experienced advisors explain to their clients how their compensation structure is beneficial to their clients. I also want to help less experienced individuals determine which compensation model is most suitable for them and the team they choose to work in. I will provide information about compensation ranges for several advisor channels and a checklist about advisor career and lifestyle goals, desired responsibilities, sources of advisor enjoyment and satisfaction, personal qualities and skill sets. I will also give my views regarding how advisor compensation structures affect the relationships between advisors and their clients.

The financial advice industry offers many different compensation structures through a variety of advice channels including brokerages, dealers, retail banks (excluding brokerages) and insurance agencies. I believe that most, if not all, compensation structures fall into essentially three categories: revenue sharing, salaried and salary plus bonus. I will describe and discuss these categories based on my experiences and my exposure to structures beyond my practice. However, compensation packages vary from firm to firm, and are constantly changing. Describing and understanding all of the variations of these compensation structures is probably not possible and is definitely beyond the scope of this book.

How you wish to be paid relates to your choices for the other business model components. If you decide that you wish to be paid a reliable consistent salary, your firm/team leader will likely have predetermined who your clients are, the services and products you will offer and the processes you will use, as well as the pricing. Conversely, if you choose to be an advisor under the revenue sharing structure, you will likely have more control and discretion regarding most aspects of your business model.

Description of Basic Compensation Structures

Salaried Advisor Compensation

A salaried advisor receives a secure, reliable, consistent income for serving a predetermined, assigned clientele. Most people are more comfortable with a reliable income than the unpredictable income of an entrepreneur or small business owner. The income of a salaried advisor for the first three to five years is likely to be considerably more than the first three to five years of the average revenue sharing advisor. However, salaried advisors' opportunities for significant long-term raises generally come from promotions to new positions or from being moved to another clientele, forcing them to abandon previous client relationships and establish relationships with new clients. Most salaried advisor positions are relieved of making the previously mentioned service model and clientele decisions as the clientele and service model will be predetermined by their firm.

Salary Plus Bonus Advisor Compensation

Under the salary plus bonus advisor compensation structure, the advisor does not share the revenue produced by the client, but they do receive bonuses that are likely based on their performance as measured by the firm's employee "scorecard". I am told these scorecards show their performance relating to product sales targets and quotas set by their firms and often include non-investment products, such as lines of credit, mortgages, credit cards, bank accounts, etc., in addition to investment products.

Revenue Sharing Advisor Compensation

I will use the term "revenue sharing" to describe the compensation of advisors who receive a predetermined (usually percentage) share of the revenue generated for the advisor's firm by the advisor's clients. However, it is worth noting that most of those advisors also pay some expenses and rightly view themselves as entrepreneurs with small businesses. Most revenue sharing advisor practices are essentially small businesses within a larger institution. This revenue sharing advisor compensation structure is usually associated with "full-service brokerage" firms; however, mutual fund dealers, insurance agencies and many financial planning and independent investment counseling/wealth management firms will also use a form of this compensation structure.

This advice channel is often still referred to as the brokerage channel; however, most advisors within the channel have evolved far beyond brokering trades to include most of the services we have discussed in the service model section of this book. As a result, former "brokerage" firms are now often referred to as full-service wealth management firms or wealth management/private client divisions of larger institutions.

Under the revenue sharing advisor compensation structure, the advisor is expected to find and serve their own clients. An advisor may take several years to build a clientele large enough to provide a good income or to determine that they should be looking at a different career path more suitable to them. Some revenue sharing advisors get their start and/or build on their business by receiving a group referral of an existing clientele upon the retirement or downsizing of their team's lead advisor. The opportunity for group referrals is earned by demonstrating the traits and attributes of a successful advisor as well as a compatibility with the particular clientele. My handbook *Transitioning Clients and the Retirement Exit Decision* discusses this topic in greater detail.

The revenue sharing advisor's earnings are increased primarily by generating more business from new and existing clients and are vulnerable to market volatility and the comings and goings of clients. The revenue generated from clients is generally split between the advisor and the firm. The percentage share received by the advisor is established by the firm in their advisor compensation package. The sharing percentage often depends on the firm's cost of providing the particular product or facilitating the particular service, as well as the size of each revenue/commission transaction and/or the size of the advisor's practice. The advisor is usually expected to share or pay some expenses for their team (salary and/or bonus, etc.) as well as some costs of marketing and developing their own practice. The revenue sharing business model allows the advisor to run their practice as a unique business-within-a-business at their firm.

Successful advisors under the revenue sharing structure have been able to enjoy long careers, long relationships with clients and continuous potential for earnings growth as they maintain and grow their practices without needing a promotion to a different role.

My practice operated under a revenue sharing compensation structure and was essentially a semi-independent business within a large Canadian Bank's wealth management/private client division.

Advisor Compensation Range

An advisor's potential earnings varies greatly with the advisor channel, their firm and the compensation structure. The information on the chart below was included in the 2019 Advisors' RC, published by *Investment Executive* newspaper, as well as in the newspaper's 2019 RC on Banks. The results were based on data that was gathered through phone surveys with 1,771 Canadian advisors in total.

Advisor's Total Annual Compensation	Brokerages	Dealers	Retail Banks	Insurance Agencies
Below $100,000	2.4%	19.9%	29.3%	25.5%
$100,000 to $250,000			63.3%	
$250,000 to $500,000			7.3%	
$100,000 to $500,000	45.2%	57.8%		56.4%
$500,000 to $1,000,000	31.6%	15.9%	0.0%	12.3%
More than $1,000,000	20.8%	6.4%	0.0%	5.8%

The advisor channels included in the survey are defined by *Investment Executive* as follows:

Brokerages: Advisors working in exclusively IIROC-registered firms (major bank-owned brokerages as well as in national and regional independents)

Dealers: Advisors who work through full-service or mutual dealers that are IIROC and/or MFDA-registered

Retail Banks (Big Six banks): Branch-based financial advisors and/or planners who are primarily paid a salary or salary with bonus

Insurance Agencies: Advisors with a primary focus on life insurance and who work with either dedicated sales agencies (where they work for that company specifically) or managing general agencies/MGAs (where they process business through the MGA)

The data from the survey indicates that the average "brokerage" channel advisors seem to have the highest income. "Appendix B: Why Many Full-Service Independent Revenue Sharing Advisors Have and Deserve Above Average Incomes" articulates my thoughts on why this is so. Many of the discussions put forth in this article will remind revenue sharing advisors of the value they bring to their clients through the long-term advisor-client relationship.

Advisor Channel Compensation Structure

I believe a very high percentage of brokerage, dealer and insurance agency advisors are revenue sharing advisors who build their clientele and control their service model, operating essentially as a business-within-a-business. The advisors in the "retail banks" channel are primarily salary or salary plus bonus and are likely required to provide other services in addition to investing and financial planning. The following excerpt from the *Investment Executive* 2019 Advisor RC would seem to show that revenue sharing advisors work primarily in the brokerage, dealer and insurance agency channels.

Average % of Source of Revenue	Brokerages	Dealers	Retail Banks	Insurance Agencies
Fee or Asset Based	74.0%	71.8%	15.0%	19.9%
Transaction Based	21.0%	24.9%	4.9%	2.8%
Fee for Service	2.2%	1.8%		0.8%
Deal Based	1.4%	0.2%		
Branch Manager Override	1.2%	1.4%		
First Year Commission				48.3%
Renewals				28.2%
Referrals			0.1%	
Bonus Based			20.6%	
Salary			59.3%	

Choosing Compensation Structure: Identification of Traits and Attributes

I have developed a checklist to help an individual identify which advisor compensation model is the best fit with who they are, their goals, ambitions and career expectations by listing many possible traits and attributes of an advisor, and indicating if the trait or attribute is usually common to revenue sharing advisors and/or salaried advisors. I used myself as an example for the sample checklists.

These traits and attributes are categorized as follows:

- Advisor career and lifestyle goals
- Desired responsibilities
- Source of advisor enjoyment and satisfaction
- Advisor personal qualities
- Advisor skill sets

After the individual has identified the traits and attributes that suit them on the checklists input tab, the checklist's template tab "Fit Comparison of Revenue Sharing Versus Salary Advisor Compensation Models" will help them to determine which compensation model will be most compatible with them and their needs. An individual looking to join the industry or change their career path can use this checklist to help them determine their compatibility with potential team leaders and firms they may wish to work with during the first or next stage of their career. For example, an individual wishing to work in an entrepreneurial setting will likely be more compatible working on a team operating within a revenue sharing compensation structure. An individual might discover very little compatibility with either model, at which point they should likely pursue a different career.

Advisor Career and Lifestyle Goals

An advisor's long-term realistic career goals should relate directly to the advisor's desired lifestyle, especially how much money the advisor aspires to earn and how much time they wish to spend working.

Advisor Career and Lifestyle Goals

x	Aspire to a lifelong career as a financial advisor
	Consider the advisor role as a stepping stone to other role in the industry
	A stable paycheque (not vulnerable to market volatility and client turnover)
x	Unlimited potential earning based on advisor's success with clients
x	Willing to accept uncertain paycheque in return for greater potential long-term income
x	Control over practice similar to having your own small business
x	Ability to choose clientele
x	Ability to build own clientele
	Work 7-8 hour days, 5 days per week
x	Willing to work long hours, especially while building clientele
x	Control over work day schedule and location

An advisor looking for the higher income and freedom associated with the revenue sharing compensation structure will need to sacrifice their time, effort and income in their early years. I remember hearing the following quote early in my career:

> *"If you work like no one else will in the beginning of your career, you can live like no one else can later on."*

The revenue sharing advisor's work schedule is generally more flexible. However, the benefit of that flexibility is usually experienced later in the advisor's career, after the successful advisor has established a team and a clientele providing a reliable revenue stream. Salaried advisors are likely to enjoy a more consistent work-life balance throughout their career.

Desired Responsibilities

Revenue sharing advisors generally desire more responsibilities, freedom and independence. Their entrepreneurial spirit enjoys the resulting challenges and control. Many successful revenue sharing advisors pay a significant portion of the costs of their team and marketing. Salaried employees generally have fewer choices and responsibilities with less control, less stress and no expenses.

Desired Responsibilities

x	Look after and advise on other people's life savings and financial well-being
x	Expect to pursue new clients
	Expect clients to be given to you
x	Choosing the specific investments from a very broad product shelf
x	Complete freedom to choose third party investments (independent from firm products)
	Like the simplicity of a smaller, more focused investment product shelf
	Like being limited to firm's own investment products
x	Don't want to be limited to firm's own investment products
x	Find unique solutions to clients' financial issues
	Like a standard short list of solutions to client problems
x	Willing to manage an assistant or team of assistants
x	Willing to pay a significant portion of the costs (team, marketing, technology, etc.)

During my last five years, I paid over 30% of my earnings towards the costs of my team. The additional responsibility, choices and control over my team increased my ability to personalize services to meet clients' unique needs and allowed me to enjoy the work-life balance I gave up in the early years of my career.

Source of Advisor Enjoyment and Satisfaction

An advisor's source of enjoyment will likely evolve over the years as they gain experience and develop professional knowledge and interests.

Source of Advisor Enjoyment and Satisfaction

x	Serving clients
x	Constant interaction with people
x	The challenge of finding unique solutions to client problems
x	Choosing investments and determining how best to react to uncontrollable events
x	A job that is always changing (no two days are ever the same)
x	Building their own clientele
x	Practice management (building team, create and modify processes)
x	Independence similar to a small business owner

Early in my career, I was most inspired by looking for new clients and picking investments. By the end of my career, I was more inspired by enjoying relationships with clients, teaching team members and improving existing services and processes.

Advisor Personal Qualities

Salaried advisors and revenue sharing advisors share many of the same qualities. Revenue sharing advisors must also possess additional entrepreneurial qualities to enable them to build their unique practice.

Advisor Personal Qualities

x	High emotional IQ: ability to empathize and relate to clients, team members and partners
x	Have and project confidence
x	Ability to accept rejection from potential and existing clients
x	Ability to handle stress from market volatility, client demands, time pressures
x	Proactive entrepreneurial attitude/mind-set compatible with a "business-within-a-business"
x	Curiosity, desire to learn (investments, tax rules, current events, financial planning, insurance)
x	Creativity and finding solutions for clients' changing needs (investments, financial planning)
x	Strong conviction regarding their own approach and overall strategies

My conviction regarding my approach and overall strategies grew over the years with my experience and success.

Advisor Skill Sets

All advisors require the basic skills in the first six skill sets listed below. The revenue sharing advisor needs the additional skill sets to enable them to build and operate their unique practice.

Advisor Skill Sets

x	Communication: face-to-face and phone calls
x	Communication: writing e-mails, letters
x	Learn and apply knowledge
x	Investing
x	Time management
x	Financial planning
x	Service model development
x	Business development/marketing
x	Practice management

Fit Comparison of Revenue Sharing Versus Salary Advisor Compensation Models

After the "Input" tab is completed, the "Fit Comparison" tab compares your chosen goals, personality and skills to those compatible with each compensation model. The shaded checkboxes on the fit comparison tab show the traits and attributes common to advisors in each compensation structure, thereby enabling you to analyze which compensation model you are most compatible with.

Revenue Sharing	Salary	Advisor Career and Lifestyle Goals
x	x	Aspire to a lifelong career as a financial advisor
		Consider the advisor role as a stepping stone to other role in the industry
		A stable paycheque (not vulnerable to market volatility and client turnover)
x		Unlimited potential earning based on advisor's success with clients
x		Willing to accept uncertain paycheque in return for greater potential long-term income
x		Control over practice similar to having your own small business
x		Ability to choose clientele
x		Ability to build own clientele
		Work 7-8 hour days, 5 days per week
x		Willing to work long hours, especially while building clientele
x		Control over work day schedule and location

Revenue Sharing	Salary	Desired Responsibilities
X	X	Look after and advise on other people's life savings and financial well-being
X		Expect to pursue new clients
		Expect clients to be given to you
X		Choosing the specific investments from a very broad product shelf
X		Complete freedom to choose third party investments (independent from firm products)
		Like the simplicity of a smaller, more focused investment product shelf
		Like being limited to firm's own investment products
X		Don't want to be limited to firm's own investment products
X		Find unique solutions to clients' financial issues
		Like a standard short list of solutions to client problems
X		Willing to manage an assistant or team of assistants
X		Willing to pay a significant portion of the costs (team, marketing, technology, etc.)

Revenue Sharing	Salary	Source of Advisor Enjoyment and Satisfaction
x	x	Serving clients
x	x	Constant interaction with people
x		The challenge of finding unique solutions to client problems
x	x	Choosing investments and determining how best to react to uncontrollable events
x	x	A job that is always changing (no two days are ever the same)
x		Building their own clientele
x		Practice management (building team, create and modify processes, etc.)
x		Independence similar to a small business owner

Revenue Sharing	Salary	Advisor Personal Qualities
x	x	High emotional IQ: ability to empathize and relate to clients, team members and partners
x	x	Have and project confidence
x	x	Ability to accept rejection from potential and existing clients
x	x	Ability to handle stress from market volatility, client demands, time pressures
x		Proactive entrepreneurial attitude/mind-set compatible with a "business-within-a-business"
x		Curiosity, desire to learn (investments, tax rules, current events, financial planning, insurance)
x		Creativity and finding solutions for clients' changing needs (investments, financial planning)
x		Strong conviction regarding their own approach and overall strategies

Revenue Sharing	Salary	Advisor Skill Sets
x	x	Communication: face-to-face and phone calls
x	x	Communication: writing e-mails, letters
x	x	Learn and apply knowledge
x	x	Investing
x	x	Time management
x	x	Financial planning
x		Service model development
x		Business development/marketing
x		Practice management

An analysis of the above "Fit Comparison of Revenue Sharing Versus Salary Advisor Compensation Models" sample reveals that I am most compatible with the revenue sharing compensation structure. The fit is most evident where I did not check many of the salary advisor shaded boxes (career and lifestyle goals, and desired responsibilities).

Client Relationships and Advisor Compensation

Some clients will be more comfortable with the compensation structure of the salaried advisor, while others will be more comfortable with the revenue sharing advisor.

Clients who are more comfortable with advisors on salary may feel they will get more objective advice from a salaried advisor than a revenue sharing advisor if the fee/commission varies between the investment choices. They may believe that a transaction-based revenue sharing advisor would be incented to make more changes to client accounts in the interest of generating more income for themselves. These clients may have lower costs with a salaried advisor, especially if they are smaller clients and would be subject to minimum fees with a revenue sharing advisor.

A client who prefers the revenue sharing advisor structure likes to know that their advisor benefits directly from any revenue earned from their accounts, as they believe it aligns the interests of the advisor more closely with the client's interests instead of the advisor's firm. These clients know their advisor will benefit or suffer from growth or losses of the clients' assets alongside the clients, especially if the clients' costs are more fee- or asset-based than transaction-based. They believe the revenue sharing advisor will be less likely to emphasize proprietary products. These clients seek a long continuous, person-to-person relationship with an advisor who is motivated to keep them happy for the length of the advisor's career. Knowing that the advisor can grow their own income significantly without having to accept a promotion that takes them away from the client reassures the client that the same advisor will be there to steer them through good and bad stock markets and be personally accountable to the client for the results of their advice.

Career Paths in Financial Advice

In today's financial advice industry, very few people step directly into the role of a financial advisor. Most people get their start by working in different entry-level roles within a financial institution as they determine their career interests. While the entry-level position is important, the industry provides the flexibility to change career paths as an individual's experience, views, knowledge and personal goals evolve.

Many of today's new financial advisors start their careers working for an established advisor, often progressing from an assistant to an associate as they gain experience thereby moving from salary, to salary plus bonus to full revenue sharing when/if they become an advisor with their own clientele. Many of these individuals are comfortable and happy remaining in the roles of assistant, assistant to associate or the associate for their entire career, never aspiring to the role of advisor/team leader and the related responsibilities. My handbook *Team Building for Financial Advisors* explores these positions in greater depth. I have also seen many of those who worked for revenue sharing advisors become salaried advisors in other channels (e.g. retail banks), and some salaried advisors move to revenue sharing channels.

Understanding the traits indicated in the checklists for choosing a compensation structure will likely help those considering a career in financial advice assess which advice channel they will be more comfortable in. I think an individual looking for a career in financial advice should pursue a position with an established financial advisor whose goals, responsibilities, qualities, skill sets and compensation structure appeal to the individual.

Appendix C includes more details from *IE*'s various 2019 Report Cards regarding the average age, experience, clientele, practices, etc. that are common in the advisors of the various advice channels. This information may provide further assistance to individuals looking to choose their career path.

An individual's goals often change as they gain experience and knowledge about the industry while expanding their personal capabilities. They will likely change their career path accordingly.

— — —

The advisor compensation model that is right for you will depend on your personal priorities relating to work-life balance, desire to personalize your business model and desired income.

The more entrepreneurial advisor will lean towards a revenue sharing compensation structure by having a completely independent practice or a "business-within-a-business" practice facilitated by the brokerage, dealer and insurance agency channels. Revenue sharing advisors generally have the freedom to operate all aspects of their practice as they see best for their unique clientele, and the potential to earn much more, but they will have to sacrifice time and income in their earlier years.

Salaried advisors usually enjoy a more stable pay cheque, have less stress and no expenses with less control over their clientele and their service model (constrained by firm policy).

Whichever compensation structure is chosen, the advisor needs to be able to explain their compensation to clients with clarity and conviction pointing out how the client benefits from the structure.

Review Your Business Model as a Whole

It is important to assess all your business model components together. They all interrelate with each other and should not be considered in isolation. For example, your selections of services should resonate with your sustainable clients, and you should not be pursuing or maintaining clients that don't need and/or appreciate your services. You also need to determine if your business model organizes your practice's services, processes, etc. to effectively and efficiently achieve your overall mission and fulfill your commitment to your clients. You may find yourself modifying your mission and/or your commitment when faced with the practicality of implementing your proposed business model.

Additional Business Model Decisions

After identifying all of the components of your business model, you should be better prepared to determine how many client households you wish to serve and the level of service you wish to provide to your clients.

Client Household Capacity

Determining how many households an advisor's practice can serve is a function of its service model, team capabilities and the efficiency and effectiveness of its processes as well as how much time the advisor has available to work. Advisors need to decide how many households they currently have the capacity to serve properly and how many households they wish to serve going forward.

In my first 15 years, I added team members to add capacity as discussed in detail in my *Team Building for Financial Advisors* handbook. Several times during my career I referred a group of my least compatible clients to other advisors more suitable for those clients. Transitioning groups of clients to another advisor is discussed thoroughly in my *Transitioning Clients and the Retirement Exit Decision* handbook for financial advisors. Advisors can add capacity by not wasting resources on services that a client does not want or need. This can be accomplished on a client by client basis or by segmenting the clientele.

Segmentation of Clientele

Many advisors consciously divide/segment their clientele into groups "A, B, C and D" usually based on the revenue generated by those clients and/or their assets. These advisors will provide different levels of service for each group. A firm can facilitate their advisors' segmentation of clientele by providing household data and rankings by various metrics, such as revenue generated, assets under management, fee-based revenue, etc. These rankings will help an advisor determine how many households would fall into each potential segment thereby helping them determine the criteria for each segment and what services they can afford to provide to each segment. Although I did not formally segment my clientele, I would rather smaller clients receive "C or D level" service from an independent advisor than no independent advice at all, so I have created some tools to help advisors wishing to segment their clientele.

Identify Your Criteria for A, B, C and D Segments of Clientele

I have created a simple template to help advisors evaluate the segments resulting from the application of potential criteria. The template and the following sample are downloadable from my website. The sample is for a fictitious advisor and is not intended as a recommended criterion.

Sample Segmenting Advisor (Advisor Name)
Identify Criteria for Segmented Clientele for Service Model
Date

Segment	Segment Criteria	# of Households	% of Total Households	Segment Revenue	% of Total Revenue	Segment AUM*	% of Total AUM*
A	Annual Revenue over $10,000	100	34%	$ 2,100,000	69%	$ 300,000,000	72%
B	Annual Revenue $5,000-$10,000	100	34%	$ 750,000	25%	$ 100,000,000	24%
C	Annual Revenue $2,000-$5,000	55	19%	$ 137,500	5%	$ 15,000,000	4%
D	Annual Revenue Under $2,000	40	14%	$ 50,000	2%	$ 3,500,000	1%
	Total	295	100%	$ 3,037,500	100%	$ 418,500,000	100%

*AUM: Assets under management

- Percentages may not equal 100% due to rounding

Create Your Segmented Clientele Service Model

To facilitate the articulation of an advisor's approach to segmenting their clientele, I have created separate checklist templates with items identical to those previously described for each service model category, including columns for four client segments. Both the template and a sample are downloadable from my website. The following is the fictitious sample summary for a segmenting advisor's client communication service model.

Segmenting Advisor Sample (Advisor Name)
Summary Of Service Model for Client Communication

	Client Segment			
	A	B	C	D
Client Contact Methods				
personal phone calls with updates	monthly	quarterly	semi-annually	annually
personal phone calls re transactions	as needed	as needed	as needed	as needed
voicemail for incoming calls	after hours only	after hours only	after hours only	after hours only
personal e-mail	as needed	as needed	as needed	as needed
face-to-face review at advisor's office	semi-annually	annually	as needed	on request
face-to-face review at client's location	as needed	on request	on request	on request
online review	as needed	as needed	as needed	on request
mailout/e-mail review	semi-annually	as needed	annually	on request
market update letters/e-mails	mass blast, quarterly	mass blast, quarterly	mass blast, quarterly	mass blast, quarterly
money manager update letters/e-mails	group blast, as needed	group blast, as needed	group blast, as needed	group blast, as needed
stock update letters/e-mails	group blast, as needed	group blast, as needed	group blast, as needed	group blast, as needed
newsletters	mass blast, quarterly	mass blast, quarterly	mass blast, quarterly	mass blast, quarterly
website postings	available to all	available to all	available to all	available to all
blogs	available to all	available to all	available to all	available to all
videos	available to all	available to all	available to all	available to all
podcasts	available to all	available to all	available to all	available to all
Client Reminders				
maturing GICs, CSBs, bonds, etc.	as needed	as needed	as needed	as needed
RRSP contributions	annually	annually	annually	annually
TFSA contributions	annually	annually	annually	annually
RESP contributions	annually	annually	annually	annually
life insurance premium reminders	annually	annually	annually	annually

Client Reminders (continued)

disability insurance premium reminders	annually	annually	annually	annually
critical illness premium reminders	annually	annually	annually	annually
RRSP conversion to RRIF/annuity	annually	annually	annually	annually
LIRA conversion to LRIF/annuity	annually	annually	annually	annually
tax loss selling	annually	annually	annually	

Personal Touches

holiday season cards	annually	annually	annually	annually
team picture	annually	annually	annually	annually
family picture	10 clients annually			
holiday season gifts	annually			
sympathy cards/gifts	as needed	as needed		
personal celebration gifts	as needed	as needed		
birthday cards/letters	annually	annually		
birthday calls	annually			
sports/entertainment tickets	annually			
individual client lunches/dinners	annually	sometimes		
individual client entertainment events	annually			
book gifts	sometimes	sometimes	sometimes	
referral thank-you calls	every referral	every referral	every referral	every referral
referral thank-you gifts	every referral	every referral	sometimes	sometimes

COMMENTS

A Clients: also included some clients with lower production but huge potential.

B Clients: also included some clients with big potential.

The contact management system provides daily team member reminders to provide service to particular clients.

The process of creating the fictitious advisor sample reaffirmed my belief in the need for a flexible service model based on the uniqueness of each client. It is also worth noting that many contact methods can be performed for all clients without much additional effort per client.

I understand the logic behind segmenting a clientele, but I was never comfortable with the idea of formally segmenting my clientele, preferring to determine the services provided to each client based on the client's needs. However, we usually did spend less time on clients with fewer assets because they had simpler needs thereby requiring less individual attention. For example, we were less likely to suggest extra customized portfolio reporting or more than two financial plan scenarios to smaller clients. Client meetings with smaller clients were generally shorter, simply because there was less to discuss. Much of our service benefited all clients without additional effort for the individual client (choosing and following managers, newsletters, process and template development, etc.).

This aversion to formally segmenting clients is due to my belief that strong relationships evolve from understanding the uniqueness of each client and providing service accordingly. I believe clients will be most comfortable with advisors who recognize, understand and respond to the client's uniqueness. A good contact management system allows the advisor to individualize the services received by each client. This may actually save advisors and clients time by preventing the unnecessary provision of particular services to clients who don't want or need that particular service.

Key Takeaways

A well-articulated, written business model is a valuable tool for advisors at all stages of their career.

Most advisors are unlikely to create a written business model because of the time it would take to do so from scratch. This book provides a quick and organized process for creating a written business model through the use of the checklists template found on my website. Using these checklists to simply record the business model of an existing practice will be fairly quick, while using the checklist to stimulate thoughts of developing or modifying a business model will take as long as the advisor's thought process needs.

Advisor firm management, regulators and industry product/ service suppliers would gain a deeper awareness of the uniqueness and needs of both advisors and advisors' clients from a thorough understanding of the components of advisors' unique business models.

The business model that is best for you will be centered around your personal convictions relating to the services you choose to offer and the clients you wish to serve. A good business model will articulate who your preferred clients are and what you will do for them. The resulting clarity will give you the focus needed to efficiently and effectively provide the services you deem appropriate to your chosen client base.

Component 1: Identify the Most Compatible Clients for Your Practice
If you feel like you are constantly bending over backwards to keep a client, you are probably not compatible and are fighting a losing battle. Let them go! You will both be happier. Relationships that satisfy many of your checklist items should be

sustainable, win-win relationships. Ultimately, you will keep the clients that are most compatible with you, and you will be working to replace those that aren't. The more compatible you are with your client, the stronger the relationship. The stronger your relationship with a client, the more likely they will take all of your advice and send you referrals. Clients will stay with you because you "get" them, and they will be your best source of new compatible clients. Your practice will be more focused, more efficient and more enjoyable for you.

Component 2: The Service Component of a Financial Advisor's Business Model

In today's world, the financial advisor's service model needs to go well beyond "robo-advisors" or discount investment service providers in order to compete. The financial advisor's services should "exceed the needs". The service must be humanized and personal, yet efficient and scalable. An advisor's efforts and services need to be visible, so the clients know they are receiving value for the fees and/or commissions paid. An advisor's unique service model should always be considered a "work in progress". An advisor who keeps up to date regarding client communication methods, investing, financial planning and taxes will find ways to constantly improve their service model.

Component 3: Processes for Streamlining Delivery of Services and Practice Management

The use of systematic processes and templates by yourself and your team will enable efficient delegation and supervision of the performance of many of the activities needed to find and service your sustainable client base and help you run your practice. This topic will be covered in more detail in my future handbook on processes and presentations.

Component 4: Determine Needed Resources and Suppliers/ Sources

Every advisor's most important resource is their own time. The other resources should be managed to maximize the use of the advisor's time. An advisor needs to determine what resources they have ready access to through their firm and external sources, including product providers, such as money managers, software providers, industry associations and independent advisor coaches. Most successful advisors have spent significant amounts of their own money on their practice. Waiting for your firm or anyone else to invest in your practice will limit your ability to grow and/or serve your clients.

Component 5: Pricing and Client Costs Model

A good pricing and client costs model will benefit all concerned. Clients and advisors should both believe that the pricing and costs are fair, thereby resulting in a sustainable, win-win relationship. With a successful pricing model, clients believe that their advisor should be paid for their effort and expertise and that they are receiving good value for their dollar. Advisors should feel they are being fairly compensated for their effort and expertise. A good pricing model will naturally align the interests of the advisor with their clients such that the advisor benefits or suffers alongside their client and that the advisor's success is contingent on the success of their client. Full transparency of all a client's fees and costs, and a clear understanding of how an advisor is paid, is crucial to the maintenance of a long sustainable relationship between the advisor and the client.

Component 6: Advisor Compensation and Career Paths

How you wish to be paid relates to your choices for the other business model components. If you decide that you wish to be paid a reliable consistent salary, your firm/team leader will likely have predetermined who your clients are, the services and products you will offer and the processes you will use, as well as the pricing. Conversely, if you choose to be an advisor compensated under the revenue sharing structure, you will likely have more control and discretion regarding most aspects of your business model. Successful advisors under the revenue sharing compensation structure have been able to enjoy long careers with long relationships with their clients and continuous potential for earnings growth as they maintain and grow their practices without needing a promotion to a different role. Whichever compensation structure is chosen, the advisor needs to be able to explain their compensation to clients with clarity and conviction pointing out how the client benefits from the structure.

It is important to assess all your business model components together. They all interrelate with each other and should not be considered in isolation. Articulating your business model should help you determine how many client households you can and/or should serve as well as the level of service you should provide each client.

The uniqueness of you and your business model is what sets you apart from other advisors and builds the loyalty amongst your clientele as they realize that no one else can be exactly like you and offer exactly what you do. The checklists and "Appendix A: Why Advisors are Not Interchangeable" should remind you of your uniqueness and give you confidence as well as provide ideas for marketing.

Final Thoughts

It is my hope that most advisors who have read this book will take the time to articulate their practice's unique business model regardless of where they are in their career. I believe the checklists tool explained in this book and downloadable from my website will make it easy to do so.

It is also my hope that this book has provided insight and a deeper understanding of practicing financial advisors to those who manage or provide services and products to advisors as well as those who aspire to be financial advisors. I believe that firms will benefit from their advisor's well developed and articulated business model. The advisor's improved focus, efficiency and effectiveness will result in better client and team member retention resulting in higher long-term revenue for the firm.

Developing the right business model is really about the advisor knowing the kind of people they enjoy working with, the work they enjoy performing and what they hope to accomplish for their clients and in their career. Your unique business model should inspire you to come to work every day and go home feeling productive, knowing that you have provided valuable services to your clients.

Afterword: COVID-19

**There is nothing like a serious crisis to
test all aspects of a business model.**

I believe financial advisors are most important during times of crises. During a crisis, clients need someone they trust to help them avoid making emotional decisions, stay the course with their investments and stick to their financial plan. Any bear market or crisis is effectively a stress test of an advisor's business model. A crisis is an advisor's opportunity to see and solve weaknesses in their practice's business model. They can discover new client needs, possibly leading to the improvements of existing services and the development of new services. It is also an opportunity to strengthen relationships and prove their value to clients. Clients will usually remember how their advisor made them feel during a crisis.

As I began the process of self-publishing the first three handbooks of this series, the world and the financial advice industry were suddenly facing the COVID-19 world pandemic health crisis. In addition to healthcare workers and people infected by the virus, the crisis dramatically affected the everyday lives and financial circumstances of a huge number of people in the world as countries closed their borders, schools, stores and restaurants, maintaining only essential services. Arts, sporting and social events around the world were canceled, and large populations were confined to their homes. Individuals, including advisors, team members and clients, faced major challenges relating to childcare and eldercare. Economic activity ground to a halt; unemployment soared to historic levels; stock markets plummeted, and many businesses struggled to survive government mandated closures. The businesses that survived had to adapt to a new world of "social distancing".

While living through this crisis, I reviewed the topics discussed in this handbook, with the effects of the crisis in mind, to point out areas where an advisor's personal business model may need to evolve due to changes brought about by COVID-19.

Compatible Clients

COVID-19 may have triggered some new client service requirements as discussed in this book's communication needs for sustainable individual relationships. A client may now require virtual meetings for health reasons, or they may have discovered they prefer the experience and saving the travel time. They may also now see a need for a personal continuity plan.

Communication Services

The need to communicate with clients is more crucial than ever during a crisis. During COVID-19, government mandated social distancing prevented all physical interaction between advisors and clients thereby affecting important communication methods, such as review meetings, seminars and social interaction. Virtual meetings became the only alternative for face-to-face encounters. Clients who had refused virtual meetings in the past became more receptive as in-person meetings became unavailable. Clients who were introduced to virtual meetings by family members became more comfortable with on camera meetings.

Several advantages of virtual meetings became more apparent to me while experiencing COVID-19. Saving travel time may result in more meetings and more (virtual) face-to-face time. The participants of virtual meetings can be easily expanded to include the client's family, team members and other professionals in addition to the advisor and the client. As clients become comfortable with virtual meetings (on camera and screen sharing) it will become easier to help them fill in documents and explain items on statements or any other reports.

Previously in this book, I mentioned that we did not use the camera feature of our online meetings. However, upon experiencing COVID-19, where physical face-to-face meetings are not possible, I now believe that at least the small talk at the beginning of a review meeting should include virtual face-to-face contact (use of cameras), solidifying the personal relationship before getting down to business. We have modified the templates on our website accordingly.

When physical distancing is relaxed, there may still be a reluctance to meet in downtown offices; and house visits may become more popular.

Investment Services
COVID-19 has given advisors the opportunity to see how their investment strategy held up during the bear market and how well it participated in the recovery. Did the investments perform as expected? Should the strategy be revised going forward?

Financial Planning Services
A new crisis often brings new opportunities to help clients. Advisors should determine what information their clientele could benefit from, gain the knowledge and provide it to their clients. For example, an advisor with many small business clients could familiarize themselves with relevant government emergency assistance programs and distribute the information accordingly.

During COVID-19, the *Investment Executive* newsletter included several articles about personal continuity plans. Perhaps this is a new service or an enhancement of existing financial planning services that advisors can explore and consider offering to help clients protect themselves from future crises.

Resources

COVID-19 may have triggered the need for access to resources not previously needed. Investments in technology, such as remote access, laptops, contact management systems, virtual meetings and internal chats, may have been necessary to allow advisors and their teams to work from home. The use of e-signatures may become more acceptable and prevalent for client documents. Regulators (IIROC) appear to have made a step in this direction by allowing the use of e-signatures early in the COVID-19 crisis. I have been told that the real estate industry has been using paperless document signing systems for a few years. Perhaps the financial services industry will be prompted by COVID-19 to do the same now that IIROC has given the green light.

Cautionary Note

The short-term success of working from home during COVID-19 may create a temptation for firms to move more staff away from the office permanently to save real estate costs and travel time. However, I believe that doing so would create many long-term weaknesses. Online virtual meetings may be quicker and more efficient, but I would not assume that all clients will be happy with this compromise forever. Some clients may wish to continue with virtual review meetings forever while others will want to return to in-person meetings as soon as it is safe to do so. Client meetings in an advisor's office provide a level of credibility and professionalism that is unmatched by a virtual meeting. In-office meetings also give the client the opportunity to interact with the entire team. Working from home removes the natural setting for the interaction and sharing of ideas amongst peers outside the team, removing a source of new business model ideas. New relationships with peers and mentors will likely be more difficult to develop, and firm culture and loyalty will be harder to establish.

———

The COVID-19 crisis has provided a stress test for every financial advisor's business model. It is an opportunity to review all your business model components, especially communication methods and needed resources, using your COVID-19 experience to identify weaknesses and potential improvements. The resulting changes you make to your business model will help you and your clients navigate through the rest of COVID-19 and future crises as well as help you solidify relationships with your clients. Those satisfied clients may result in increased referrals of potential clients whose advisors failed to meet expectations during the crisis.

Appendix A:

Why Advisors are Not Interchangeable

Business is understandably always looking for the efficiencies brought about by finding the one product that fits all. However, in the advice business, recognizing that all clients are different and one advisor does NOT fit all is crucial to success. In fact, it is the flexibility of allowing advisors to be different and facilitating that difference that will allow clients to find an advisor that suits them and thereby allows a firm to serve the large variety of clients that exist today. One of my long-standing clients told me, "I always felt that you and your team always had my best interests at heart; everyone is different; it is important to understand the individual's needs, not one size fits all".

I have always believed that a client needs to be comfortable with the advisor, the strategy and individual investments in order to be a successful investor. During my 33 years in the investment industry, I realized that my well-diversified, patient approach to investing was compatible with many, but not compatible with everyone. Some clients wanted to be more aggressive than I was recommending, and—contrary to my approach—some clients wanted to engage in market timing with top-down asset allocation decisions (by asset class, by industry or by country). Sometimes our personalities were simply incompatible for unknown reasons. Often both the client and I would recognize these differences, and the relationship could end amicably. From time to time, I would suggest that a client leave me for a more compatible advisor.

Advisors are not interchangeable because:

1) Clients are unique

2) Advisors are unique

3) Advisor service models are unique

4) Good client-advisor relationships are developed over time and built on trust

There are as many unique personalities, situations and capabilities as there are clients and advisors. This uniqueness is demonstrated by the many choices illustrated in my business model checklists. I have identified below some different characteristics of clients, advisors and advisor service models to show the need for many different advisors to serve the many different needs of the many different clients. I do this in hopes of dispelling the notion that a "standard" advisor can best serve the needs of all clients and thereby prove that advisors are not interchangeable.

Clients' Distinguishing Characteristics and Needs

- personality (loud vs quiet, excited vs calm, emotional vs detached, reserved vs friendly)
- age, employment, business owner, marital status, culture, dependents, disabled dependents
- elderly family members to take care of
- if elderly themselves, do they have someone to look after them
- desire for a long-term person-to-person relationship with one financial advisor who knows their history and aspirations
- level of contact desired
- preferred method of communication (phone, in person, e-mail, mail)
- tax situation
- desire for financial planning
- desire to leave a legacy vs spending/distributing wealth during lifetime

- desire for seminars and education
- desire to train/teach their children
- level of interest in the details of recommended investments
- level of involvement in selection of specific investments
- desire to choose and hold some of their own investment ideas
- desire for someone to bounce ideas off
- ability to understand the complexity of investments
- desire for continuous new investment ideas
- desire for the latest, newest investment product
- desire for sophisticated investment ideas (including use of derivatives)
- level of comfort with risk and volatility
- ability to be patient with volatile markets

Advisors' Distinguishing Characteristics

- personality (loud vs quiet, excited vs calm, emotional vs detached, reserved vs friendly)
- willingness to listen to seemingly unrelated conversations
- completed voluntary, specialty courses as well as other degrees and designations
- ability and desire to work with and/or teach unsophisticated investors
- level of patience for beginner questions
- ability and desire to work with and find answers for sophisticated investors
- level of patience for clients asking about an idea they read about in the paper or heard about from a neighbour or at a cocktail party

- courage to disagree with a client when doing so is in the client's best interests (even when the advisor will be worse off)
- risk profile (some advisors more drawn to risky investments)
- investment philosophy (level and type of diversification, approach to asset allocation, etc.)
- **investment** knowledge, experience and willingness to recommend particular investment types:
  - cash equivalents: high interest savings accounts, money market funds, etc.
  - fixed income: government bonds, GICs, corporate bonds, preferred shares
  - stocks, ETFs, options, derivatives, structured products
  - global and international investments
  - abilities to trade in overseas markets
  - tax effective investments
  - "alternative" investments (private equity, hedge funds, etc.)
  - private placements
  - third-party managed money (multiple managers for different asset classes, industries, investment styles and/or geographic regions)
  - separately managed accounts
  - mutual funds
  - ability and desire to do own due diligence on money managers (possibly see or meet in person)
  - qualified to manage accounts on a discretionary basis
- **financial planning** knowledge and experience in:
  - goal setting including saving and spending estimates

- – planning and forecasting for retirement
- – estate planning (powers of attorney, trusts and wills)
- – insurance (life, disability, critical illness)
- – personal, corporate and estate taxes and how various investments affect them
- – issues relating to particular professions or businesses
- **tax** knowledge and experience in:
  - – preparation of tax returns
  - – strategies for tax reduction
  - – tax effect of various investments
  - – tax effect of various account types (registered accounts, etc.)

Advisor Service Model Characteristics

- – frequency and method of contact (phone, emails, mailings, meetings)
- – length of time spent with clients
- – face-to-face contact (advisor's office or client's home)
- – ability to identify and customize the reports clients receive to give them exactly the information they are looking for with the desired level of complexity/simplicity (Firms often have many reports available but won't automatically send them to all clients because no one wants all of the reports.)
- – use of financial plans (presentation format, use of graphs, multiple scenarios, update frequency, incorporate into everyday advice and/or extra cost to client?)
- – willingness and ability to work with a client's other professionals (estate lawyers and tax accountants)
- – assistance gathering and preparing information for tax preparation

- fees (transactional and/or fee-based)
- offers accounts managed on a discretionary basis
- periodic newsletters or updates
- periodic seminars for clients and/or guests

Clearly, there is an infinite number of permutations and combinations of client circumstances, personalities and needs. No advisor can develop and maintain the skill set necessary to provide all the above services, and no client wants all of these services. No advisor can be compatible with all client personalities. Clients have the right to seek out an advisor that suits their investment philosophy and service requirements in order to reach the level of comfort they need for financial peace of mind. Likewise, many advisors want the right to develop their own investment philosophy, choose which clients they service and how they service them.

Good Relationships are Developed Over Time

Finding a truly compatible advisor is a challenge. A good relationship is to be cherished and protected. Clients should have the right and opportunity to develop a long-term relationship with such an advisor. Trusting relationships take time to develop and are not readily interchangeable. The "business-within-a-business" model of the revenue sharing advisor promotes long advisor careers and provides the flexibility and earnings potential that inspires the entrepreneurial, revenue sharing advisor to develop their own particular skill sets, service model and investment strategies that attracts and pleases compatible clients.

Clients Confirm Advisors are Not Interchangeable

I received over 100 comments/letters/e-mails from clients upon my retirement. The comments revealed what the clients appreciated most about my practice and the services we offered.

A large percentage of the comments referred to the quality and length of their relationship with myself and my team.

> *"The world is too impersonal. I like that when I phone your office, you know me and my situation immediately versus all of the phone centers that companies use today. I did not have to go through numerous steps of phone menus.... Everyone has a "know your client" form or information, but you and your team really know the client."*
>
> —a client of over 20 years

Clients' actions tell a similar story. When a revenue sharing advisor leaves to go to a new firm, they ask most of their clients to follow. In order to follow their advisor, the client will suffer many inconveniences. The client will need to provide numerous signed documents to the advisor's new firm to create new accounts and transfer the contents of their existing accounts to the new firm. They will have to learn new statements/reports, electronic access systems, tax reporting systems, etc. They may have to sell or leave behind some proprietary investments that are not transferable or that the new firm can't hold. They may suffer delays when some of the portfolio is with the new firm while the rest remains with the old firm or is in transit. In spite of all of these inconveniences, I have been told that 70-95% of client assets and a marginally higher percentage of revenue will follow their revenue sharing advisor to their new firm.

Clearly clients value their person-to-person relationship with their advisor and DO NOT view advisors as interchangeable.

———

Freedom of choice for both clients and advisors results in mutually beneficial advisor-client relationships that last decades and often into the client's next generation. These person-to-person, compatible long-term relationships lead to peace of mind for all involved.

Appendix B:

Why Many Full-Service Independent Revenue Sharing Advisors Have and Deserve Above Average Incomes

For the purposes of this article, an independent revenue sharing (RS) advisor is an advisor who is expected to find and choose their own clients and make their own servicing decisions regarding communication, investment selection/recommendations, financial planning, etc. The advisor essentially operates their practice as a separate business or a business within the business of a larger institution (brokerage/wealth management firms/bank divisions, mutual fund dealers, financial planning firms, etc.). They will share in the revenue from clients and will pay some or all of the expenses of the practice. An independent advisor has a broad product shelf including non-proprietary investment products and is not expected to favour proprietary products.

I would agree that many RS advisors have above average incomes. A RS advisor needs to be able to take their own distinguishing characteristics and develop their unique service model to suit the distinguishing characteristics and needs of the clients they are compatible with, all while trying to build a clientele and keeping up to date with current investment opportunities and financial planning issues. This is very difficult to do. As a result, a very low percentage of RS advisors survive and thrive in this very competitive business. When I started, we were told that half of my fellow rookie advisors would not make it through their first year—they were right. Many advisors continued to leave after failing to build a large enough clientele within their first three or so years. Advisors who survive in the business have an extremely wide range of personal incomes based on the size of their clientele and the expenses relating to their practice. There are many reasons why this is true, and why it is justified.

Factors Determining RS Advisor Income

1) personal effort
2) personal qualities
3) skill sets
4) experience (length of career)
5) client's willingness to pay for advice
6) competition of firms for successful advisors

Personal Effort

The amount of personal effort is likely the most important factor in the RS advisor's success. Personal effort is required to develop and implement the skill sets mentioned below. A strong work ethic is a common trait amongst the advisors with the highest income. Many RS advisors will choose to work long hours and weekends, especially during the early years of their career.

Personal Qualities

- enjoy constant interaction with people
- proactive, entrepreneurial attitude and mind-set in line with a "business-within-a-business" approach
- enjoy the intellectual challenge of finding solutions to client problems, choosing investments and determining how best to react to uncontrollable events
- curiosity and desire to learn new things, constantly thinking of new questions to ask regarding investments, tax rules, current events, market history, insurance and financial planning, etc.

- creativity in finding solutions to changing client needs in the constantly shifting worlds of investment opportunities and financial planning issues
- enjoy a job that is always changing (No two days are ever the same.)
- strong conviction regarding their own approach and overall strategies relating to investments and financial matters
- ability to accept rejection from potential and existing clients
- ability to handle stress from:
    - uncontrollable and unpredictable stock markets and world events
    - the responsibility of dealing with clients' life savings
    - answering to clients for investment results
    - time pressure caused by continuous demands from clients, management and regulators
    - back office errors beyond advisor's control

Skill Sets Contributing to the Success of RS Advisors

My experience has taught me that each successful advisor has developed a unique combination of a variety of skill sets that works for their clients. An advisor's personal qualities will often determine which skill sets they choose to develop most fully.

Investment, Financial Planning and Tax Knowledge and Experience
See the many potential investment, financial planning and tax knowledge and experience items mentioned in "Appendix A: Why Advisors are Not Interchangeable" in the section "Advisors' Distinguishing Characteristics". Much of this knowledge is in addition to multiple required and voluntary industry courses as well as professional designations and post-secondary degrees

completed by the advisor. Advisors need to be continuously learning to maintain up-to-date knowledge.

People Skills
- ability to develop and maintain long-term relationships with clients, team members and other professionals
- ability to empathize and understand clients (put themselves in the client's shoes)
- ability to feel and project empathy, confidence, trustworthiness and professionalism
- ability to relate to people from many walks of life including clients, management and other professionals
- ability to relate and talk to people possessing various levels of knowledge
- communication skills: face-to-face, phone calls, writing (emails, letters, newsletters)

Service Model Development Skills
- ability to create a unique, yet efficient, service model that is customizable in response to individual client needs

Business Development/Marketing Skills
- develop and implement strategies to promote referrals and find new clients
- ability to host events or seminars to attract new clients
- creation of practice promotional materials (mailouts, etc.)
- website development
- social prospecting
- social media prospecting

Practice Management Skills

- ability to design and implement processes to provide efficient client service (use of repeatable processes, such as templates, calculators and graphs)

- design client friendly presentations that resonate with their client base

- time management (There is never enough time to do everything. They need to prioritize and leverage time as much as possible.)

- ability to delegate and outsource where possible

- team management: hire, inspire, train, motivate

Experience - Higher Pay Justified for Successful Advisors with Long Careers

Successful RS advisors usually have long careers because they have the opportunity to grow their income continuously until they retire. Generally, more experience means a higher income as the advisor's clientele grows in size and revenue. There are many reasons why more clients are willing to pay the experienced financial advisor. Five obvious reasons are that the experienced advisor:

- has experienced volatile market cycles, bubbles and crashes.

- has endured and learned from multiple past bear markets.

- has learned to temper client enthusiasm and avoid overzealous risk-taking during bull markets.

- is more likely to spot the weaknesses and dangers in the "latest and greatest" investment or planning idea because they have seen many ideas fail dramatically over the years.

- is better equipped with solutions to help clients navigate through difficult and complex personal financial issues as the advisor has likely encountered the same or similar issues with other clients.

Clients Decide What Their Advisor is Worth to Them

A person possessing a high degree of many of the above skills and qualities is relatively rare, so when an advisor is good at most of the above skills, more clients are willing to pay for their service and advice. The revenue sharing advisor and the client discuss and negotiate the client's cost of their advice. Ultimately, the clients are deciding that their advisor is worth the cost. As a result, some advisors are paid considerably more than others as more and larger clients have chosen to work with them, thus explaining and justifying the wide range of take-home pay of individual RS advisors.

Firms Compete for Advisors

Successful RS advisors are usually in high demand amongst firms because their clients want to work with the particular advisor and will usually follow the RS advisor if they move to another firm. This high demand is evidenced by the willingness of firms to compete for successful, experienced advisors by offering financial incentives to particular advisors to change firms. The knowledge of this healthy competition results in firms looking to attract and keep advisors by improving support for advisors through facilitating the advisors' ability to serve their clients. The firms do this by providing more product choice, quality research, better IT systems and efficient back offices, etc.

The laws of supply and demand and fair competition have led to above average income for many RS advisors. The supply of RS advisors is limited because of the work ethic, personal qualities and various skill sets required to succeed. Demand is provided by clients looking for long-term relationships with quality, experienced advisors and the institutions who wish to provide those clients with the advisors they desire.

Appendix C:

The Average Advisor of Various Financial Advice Channels
(data from *IE*'s 2019 Report Card Series)

Average	Brokerages	Dealers	Retail Banks	Insurance Agencies
Age	51.1	53.1	41.4	48.2
Years With Firm	13.1	11.2	13.2	9.8
Years In Industry	22.3	21.8	16.5	18.4
Assets Under Management (AUM)	$176.7 mill	$48.6 mill	$121.0 mill	$41.9 mill
Number of Households	193.1	208.2	262.9	522.4
AUM per Household	$1,082,771	$322,859	$483,390	
Female Advisor	18.4%	19.3%	39.4%	23.5%
Male Advisor	81.6%	80.7%	60.6%	76.5%

% of Client Households with AUM of	Brokerages	Dealers	Retail Banks	Insurance Agencies
Less than $100,000	6.1%	24.7%	7.4%	
$100,000 to $250,000	10.7%	23.4%	21.7%	
$250,000 to $500,000	18.1%	22.8%	27.9%	
$500,000 to $1,000,000	26.7%	17.4%	29.4%	
$1,000,000 to $2,000,000	20.4%	7.1%	10.0%	
More than $2,000,000	17.9%	4.9%	3.6%	

Average % of Source of Revenue	Brokerages	Dealers	Retail Banks	Insurance Agencies
Fee Or Asset Based	74.0%	71.8%	15.0%	19.9%
Transaction Based	21.0%	24.9%	4.9%	2.8%
Fee For Service	2.2%	1.8%		0.8%
Deal Based	1.4%	0.2%		
Branch Manager Override	1.2%	1.4%		
First Year Commission				48.3%
Renewals				28.2%
Referrals			0.1%	
Bonus Based			20.6%	
Salary			59.3%	

Average % of Product Distribution	Brokerages	Dealers	Retail Banks	Insurance Agencies
Equities	39.6%	3.5%		
Income Trusts		0.1%		
Bonds	13.5%	0.5%		
GICs			21.9%	
Term Deposits			2.2%	
PPNS (principle protected notes)			1.2%	
High Interest Savings			4.4%	
Mutual Funds	26.4%	67.4%	27.7%	40.5%
ETFs	7.6%	1.9%		
Third-Party Managed Products	3.3%	3.7%	5.6%	30.2%
Proprietary Managed Products	1.9%	4.4%	37.2%	29.3%
Alternative Investments	2.0%	0.3%		
Banking Products	3.7%	1.9%		
Insurance Products		16.7%	0.0%	
Other	2.0%			

Advisor's Total Annual Compensation	Brokerages	Dealers	Retail Banks	Insurance Agencies
Below $100,000	2.4%	19.9%	29.3%	25.5%
$100,000 to $250,000			63.3%	
$250,000 to $500,000			7.3%	
$100,000 to $500,000	45.2%	57.8%		56.4%
$500,000 to $1,000,000	31.6%	15.9%	0.0%	12.3%
More than $1,000,000	20.8%	6.4%	0.0%	5.8%

Footnotes for Data

– Percentages may not equal 100% due to rounding.

– Seven of the dealers from 2019 had both IIROC and MFDA arms, meaning they operate more similarly to their brokerage counterparts than those that don't have IIROC arms—overall, all respondents for the Dealers' RC must have derived at least half of their business from selling investment products and had at least an MFDA license.

– *Investment Executive* (*IE*) did not include Bank of Nova Scotia in the 2019 RC on Bank results for AUM and household data, due to differences in their back office. All advisors had MFDA licenses.

- AUM and household data wasn't provided for insurance advisors for 2019 (and going forward) because these advisors don't focus on investments.

- The insurance advisor average revenue data excludes advisors from RBC Life Insurance since they are salaried.

- Overall, these data points are reflective of *IE*'s interviews with individual advisors from firms across the industry. The main focus is a satisfaction survey, but the newspaper does ask for demographic information. It's possible that the self-reported book and client averages collected may not match data from the firms themselves.

Acknowledgements

My husband, Adrian Bannister, has been wonderfully encouraging and supportive of me in all my endeavours through the last 17 years of my career and the years it has taken me to write these handbooks. He has put up with my moods during stressful periods as an advisor, (the financial crisis comes to mind), as well as the trials and tribulations of my learning the process of writing and publishing these books. He has been a valuable sounding board and served as a test reader, editor and technical advisor. Adrian sometimes remembered important topics, issues and things I did during my career that I neglected to include in my early drafts. I feel very fortunate and thankful for his many contributions to my life and career.

I was extremely fortunate when a former associate of mine, Mike Bishop, agreed to work part-time with me to assist me with these books. He worked on my team for 18 years before I retired from my financial advice practice. Mike served as my editor, tech expert and sometimes as my memory and co-writer. I will be forever grateful for his help.

My practice's clients provided me with many of the ideas discussed in this book through their questions, requests and by sharing their life and business experiences with me. Thank you for all of your support and wonderful conversations throughout my career.

I have been very fortunate to draw upon many friends and contacts in the financial services industry while in the process of writing and publishing these handbooks. Many of these people served as test readers and editors, sometimes helping me to remember topics or issues that I needed to address in the books. Others simply provided much needed encouragement for me to share my experience and knowledge. I have listed the names in alphabetical order: Sonia Baxendale, John-Paul Bernardi, Rob Blagojevic, Laura Cameron, Rose Cammareri, Sandy Cardy, Dianne Carruthers, Susan Carson, Jonathan Carter, James Collins, Cindy Crean, Megan Deeks, Wilma Ditchfield, Dan Downing, Stephen Dunn, Tim Eastwood, Carole Foster, Steve Geist, Monique Gravel, Rollie Guenette, Tony Johnson, Mark Kalichman, Katie Keir, Steven Krupika, Mara Ladico, Christine Lam, Grace Lutfy, Carol Lynde, Rod Mahrt, Paul Maranger, Gaelan Martin–Timms, Gary Mayzes, Jeff McCartney, B.K. Milne, Bruce Moore, Paul Musson, Katie Ophelders, Gabby Pulcini, Kevin Punshon, Jerry Rawlik, Meri Rawling-Taylor, Ann Richards, Tammie Rix, Stephanie Sienko, Mark Slater, Lois Smith, Sean Struthers, Iris Sugiyama, Rory Tufford, Timothy Tufford, Maili Wong.

Thanks to Ryan Levesque for his patience and advice while guiding me through the self publishing process.

Thanks to Melissa Levesque for her patience and help designing the covers and the formatting of the various forms of this handbook.

About the Author

Personal Background

Christine Timms was born into a family of small business owners, the youngest of five children all born within six years. She worked several part-time jobs as a teenager as she grew up in a small town in Southern Ontario, Canada. She put herself through university thanks, in large part, to the co-op work/study program at the University of Waterloo. Christine was always very competitive in sports, school and business, never shying away from a challenge. She is a lifelong fan of the Toronto Raptors, the Toronto Blue Jays, the Buffalo Bills and Canadian tennis players. Christine lives in Toronto, Canada with her husband and son.

Financial Services Career

As Christine began to understand herself more in the early years of her professional career, she realized that she needed to see a direct relationship between her efforts and success. She wanted to be her own boss and build her own business with no glass ceiling. She had always been curious about investing, was interested in teaching and enjoyed working with people. Christine wanted the freedom to think for herself and give independent advice to clients she could work with continuously over the life of her career. Christine had a competitive nature and sought an opportunity to be judged based on quantifiable results, effectively eliminating the glass ceiling. Christine determined the best opportunity to combine these interests and goals was through the career of a full-service investment advisor.

Christine was hired and trained by Merrill Lynch Canada in 1983. She began her career as an advisor with no clients after working for three years as an internal auditor for the Canadian Federal Government. She became an advisor at CIBC Wood Gundy when they bought Merrill Lynch Canada in 1990 and remained with CIBC Wood Gundy until retirement.

- Christine achieved chairman's club in her firm for the first time in 1993 and every year thereafter during her career (24 years in a row) including 2016, her last year as an advisor. Chairman's club included the top performers of the firm (usually approximately the top 8% of the firm's advisors).

- Christine served on CIBC Wood Gundy's Retail Advisory Board (committee of advisors assembled to provide feedback to firm management) from November 1995 to September 1999.

- Christine retired December 1, 2016 after 33 years as an investment advisor with career highs in both assets under management ($400 million) and annual revenue generated. Upon retirement, Christine's clientele consisted of about 350 households, with over a third of those households having over $1,000,000 in assets under management with Christine and her team. The clientele included people from all walks of life and occupations: professionals, small business owners, public service workers, skilled trade workers, retirees, widows, etc. Almost all clients were located in the Greater Toronto Area.

Educational History
1980 Bachelor of Mathematics (B. Math)
1982 Certified Management Accountant (CMA, CPA)
1983 Canadian Securities Course (CSC), options
1993 Chartered Investment Manager (CIM)
1995 Life Insurance and Accident & Sickness Insurance Licence
2000 Professional Financial Planning (PFP)
2010 Registered Retirement Consultant (RRC)
2015 Certified Executor Advisor (CEA)

Christine no longer holds any licence to practice as a financial advisor.

Books by Christine Timms

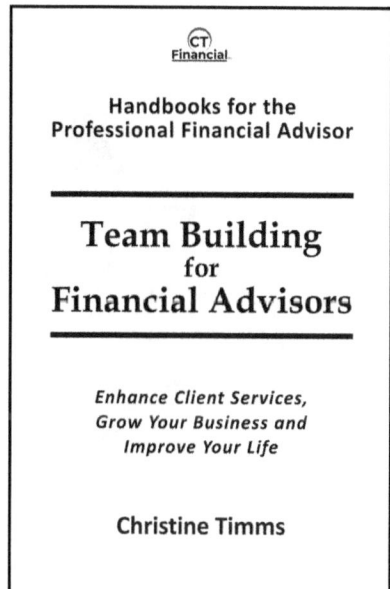

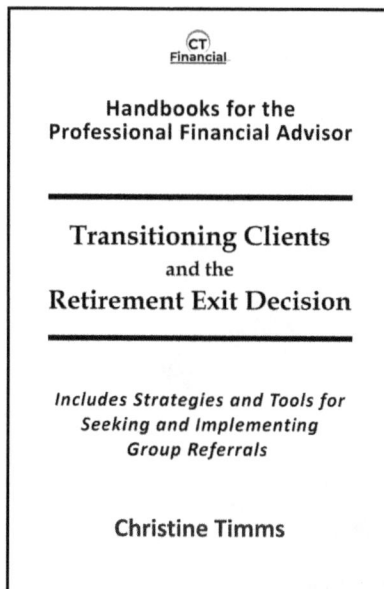

Handbooks for the Professional Financial Advisor

Business Models
for
Financial Advisors

*Develop and Articulate Your
Unique Business Model*

Christine Timms

Handbooks for the Professional Financial Advisor

Team Building
for
Financial Advisors

*Enhance Client Services,
Grow Your Business and
Improve Your Life*

Christine Timms

Handbooks for the Professional Financial Advisor

Transitioning Clients
and the
Retirement Exit Decision

*Includes Strategies and Tools for
Seeking and Implementing
Group Referrals*

Christine Timms

Templates Available on www.christinetimms.com

Business Models for Financial Advisors

Identify the Most Compatible Clients for Your Practice checklists
- Identify Compatible Groups of Clients and Potential Clients
- Identify Criteria for Sustainable Individual Relationships

Articulate Your Unique Service Model checklists
- Client Communication
- Investing
- Financial Planning
- Tax Strategies and Return Preparation

Determine Needed Resources and Suppliers checklists

Establish Pricing and Client Costs Model checklists

Choose Advisor Compensation Structure and Career Path checklists

Segmenting Clientele - Segmentation Criteria worksheet

Segmented Clientele Unique Service Model checklists

Client Investment Allocation Decision Flow Chart (free)

Team Building for Financial Advisors

Team Payroll Sensitivity Analysis spreadsheet

Advisor Actual Team Compensation Costs spreadsheet

Team Member Duty Distribution List - Associate Structure

Team Member Duty Distribution List - Specialist Structure

Transitioning Clients and the Retirement Exit Decision

Business Model Checklists (as shown in Business Models for Financial Advisors)

Steps of Transition Timeline checklist (free)

Potential Successor(s) Evaluation worksheet (free)

Sample Retirement Phone Call Script (free)

Sample Formal Retirement Letter (free)

www.ingramcontent.com/pod-product-compliance
Lightning Source LLC
Chambersburg PA
CBHW071552210326
41597CB00019B/3206